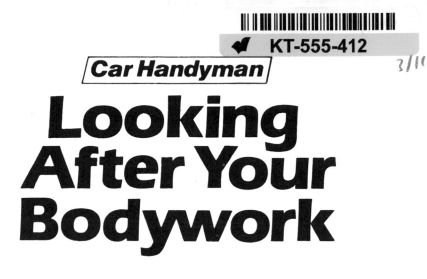

Car Handyman

Looking After Your Bodywork

Marshall Cavendish

CONTENTS

Editor Fred Milson
Designer Chris Walker
Production Controller Steve Roberts
Typesetting ABM Typographics Limited, Hull

Produced by Marshall Cavendish Books Limited
58 Old Compton Street
London W1V 5PA

ISBN 0 86307 354 9

Printed and bound in Milan, Italy by New Interlitho

INTRODUCTION

Unsightly bumps, dents and rust holes are bound to spoil your car's appearance and lower its resale value. *Looking After Your Bodywork* shows you how to tackle the problem. It explains how to repair dents and chips, how to deal with rust and how to respray your car so it comes up looking as good as new. Plus special sections on rustproofing, undersealing and repairs to door locks

Fixing faulty door locks

Door and boot locks — vital to your car's security — can be repaired or renewed with a few simple tools

Faulty door locks are not only a nuisance but may also put the security of your car and its contents at risk. Worn or faulty lock mechanisms can either make your car door hard to open or can have the opposite effect — allowing the lock to be opened with virtually any other car key — or even a flat-bladed screwdriver.

The lock and key are just two parts of a fairly complex assembly also consisting of the interior and exterior door handles, the interior lock button or knob, the door catch and the linkage which connects all these together. A fault with any one of these components can cause the whole mechanism to give problems.

When to do this job
When door locks are difficult to operate or doors cannot be locked or unlocked

What this job involves
Maintaining locking mechanism
Removing locking mechanism components
Renewing components of locking system
Refitting locking mechanism

Points to watch
Do you need special tools to fit the bolts on the striker plate? Has the door dropped on its hinges? Is this causing the problem rather than the door locks?

To do this job
Tools: Screwdrivers; spanners; pliers; torch
Materials: New components of locking system (maybe); aerosol lubricant; graphite powder; petroleum jelly
Time: Up to two hours for each door
Degree of difficulty: Working in confined spaces inside the door can be awkward

If you have the job professionally done . . .
Do door locks now work smoothly? Can car be locked and unlocked without difficulty? Has door trim been replaced neatly?

Door lock mechanisms are designed to last for a long time with a minimum of maintenance. The most important thing is to make sure that the striker plate is adjusted correctly for height and tightness. Coat the striker plate lightly with Vaseline or a recommended grease at major service intervals. Regular lubrication of the rest of the assembly is not usually easy since all the main components are located inside the door and can only be reached after the trim panel has been removed. If the lock mechanism starts to give trouble, or has been in use for a long time, the catch assembly should be removed, cleaned and lubricated. You may be able to reach inside the door with an aerosol lubricant and lubricate some of the lock assembly.

The key mechanism will benefit from a light application of fine graphite powder. This can be worked all the way into the lock by putting powder on

1. Lubricating striker plate with grease

the key and then sliding the key in and out of the lock (**fig 2**). Do not use oil to lubricate the lock as this will attract grit and dirt.

Sometimes, in extremely low temperatures, door locks can freeze, making it impossible to turn the key. If this ever happens, do not be tempted to force the key — it will probably snap off in the lock. Instead, use one of the proprietary lock de-icers that are on the market to free up the mechanism.

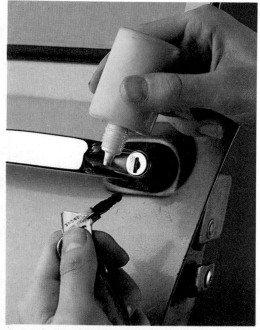

2. Applying graphite powder to key

3. Using special lock oil in key barrel

To repair a faulty door handle you will almost certainly have to remove the inner trim panel before anything can be done. The only problems which can be solved without having to do this concern either the flap-type door release jamming midway, or the push-button type either protruding too far or jamming when pushed in.

The problem of the flap type catch release jamming usually occurs when the handle is accidentally locked in the midway position — that is, when you locked or unlocked the door while you still had the flap slightly raised. Moving the key around in the barrel will usually release the handle.

A problem which can develop in some cars with push button exterior door handles is that, after a period of use, the buttons gradually start to work their way out of the door handles. All this means is that

1. Tightening push button

the bolt which holds the button in place has loosened up and needs tightening. Often this bolt can just be seen if you wind down the window, press the button about halfway inwards and look down inside the door, between the window glass and the handle. Carefully reaching inside the door with an open-ended spanner will sometimes allow you to tighten this bolt until the button goes back to its normal position.

Button releases which stick inside the door handle usually do so because the button itself needs oiling. A drop of oil or WD-40 should make it go back to its normal position and keep it working smoothly. If the button also houses the door lock, try putting the key in the lock and pulling the button out. If this does not work, the inner panel will have to be removed so that a more thorough investigation of the problem can be made.

Undo the window winder, prise the trim away from the door with a blunt screwdriver and once you have done this, peel away the polythene lining which is usually stuck to the inside of the door — you may only have to peel away one corner in order to reach the access hole next to the door handle, but on some cars it may be easier to remove it completely. Once you can reach the mechanism you can find the problem.

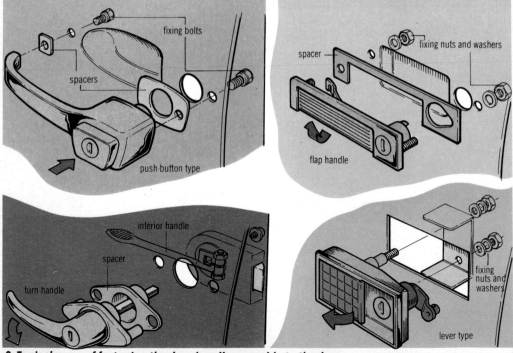

fixing bolts

spacers

push-button type

spacer

fixing nuts and washers

flap handle

interior handle

spacer

turn handle

fixing nuts and washers

lever type

2. Typical ways of fastening the door handle assembly to the door

Ask someone to operate the outer door handle while you peer inside the door with a torch to check whether the handle is operating the linkage which connects it to the catch mechanism. If nothing happens when the handle is moved, then the handle must be faulty and you will have to remove it.

First, reach inside the door and disconnect the rod which is attached to the handle mechanism. Often this is a push-fit ball and socket arrangement and the metal or nylon socket on the link rod can be pulled away either by hand or by using a pair of pliers. On other cars you may find that a clip holds the link to the inside of the handle and that this clip has to be prised away (see Step 5). It is also quite common for the door handle to operate the catch mechanism directly — the door button pushes against a lever on the catch. If this is the case the two components are positioned very close to one another and there is no linkage between them.

The door handle itself is usually held to the door by two nuts, bolts or screws and manufacturers usually leave enough room to get a screwdriver or socket inside the door. In some cases you may have to use a long extension on your socket spanner to reach the nut or bolt. The door handle assembly can then be lifted away — note that there is usually a rubber gasket fitted between the handle and the door.

There is little that you can do to overhaul a faulty door handle. The only practical solution is to either buy a new component or to find one in a breaker's yard. If the handle also contains the door lock, it may be possible to fit the original lock to the assembly so that you can continue using the original set of keys (see Step 6). Check with your dealer to find out whether this is possible with your car.

Door locks

The central component is the catch mechanism which holds the door closed. This mechanism is operated by either the interior or exterior door handle. The handle releases the catch so that the door is released from the striker plate. The catch can also be locked by either an external key-operated lock or by an internal knob or lever.

The design of these individual parts varies from one manufacturer to another although their basic method of operation is usually the same. The catch mechanism is a small but fairly complex arrangement of levers and springs mounted inside the door. The only part of the assembly which is visible is the catch itself which protrudes from the side of the door and engages with a striker plate fixed to the car body — together these hold the door closed.

The door handles themselves have changed a lot since the days of simple old-fashioned levers. Exterior handles now incorporate either a push-button or flap type release which disengages the catch. Interior handles vary even more widely, but usually consist of a small lever mounted flush with the interior door trim or the arm rest. Whichever type of lever you have, its function is to pull a rod which runs along inside the panel and activates the catch mechanism. Sometimes the interior handle also doubles as an internal door lock and moves another rod up and down inside the door panel to operate the lock lever on the catch mechanism.

The final component is the exterior lock. This may be a separate component with its own linkage to the catch mechanism or it may be part of the exterior door handle mechanism. Although there are now a few cars on the road fitted with door locks which are linked to a sophisticated alarm system all of which is activated by individually coded electrical signals, most cars still rely on a more conventional security arrangement. The key fits into the barrel of the lock and, when turned, operates a lever inside the door panel. This locks or unlocks the catch mechanism.

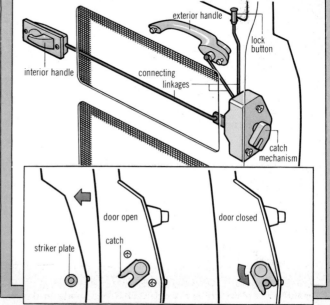

exterior handle

lock button

interior handle

connecting linkages

catch mechanism

striker plate

catch

door open

door closed

Begin by checking that the lever assembly is firmly attached to the door. Sometimes the fixing screws can work their way loose so that, on some models, the handle assembly moves instead of the rod which connects the handle to the catch mechanism. If this has happened, simply retighten the fixing screws.

A more common cause of a faulty inner door handle is that the rod which is connected to it and runs along the inside of the door has somehow freed itself from the handle. This can be checked by unscrewing the door handle from the door trim and carefully pulling the handle away until the lever on the inside can be seen (**fig 1**). If you can see that the linkage has become disconnected you may find that it is possible to fit it back into place. If it is the type which simply hooks into a hole in the

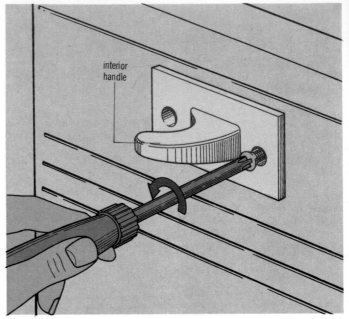

1. Unscrewing the interior door handle

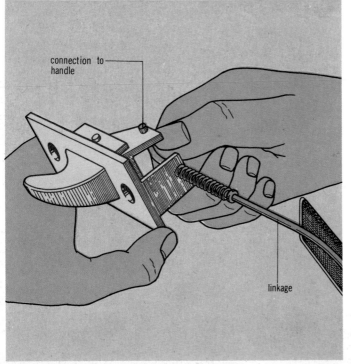

2. Hooking the linkage back into the handle

lever try juggling the handle around to hook the linkage back into place (**fig 2**). You will probably find that the inner panel has to be removed so that this can be done — especially if the rod is held in place by a clip.

It is also possible that the linkage has become disconnected from the catch mechanism. If this has happened you may be able to reach the fault by just detaching one half of the inner trim, but in most cases you will have to remove the entire trim to gain clear access to the catch mechanism. Reconnect the rod, making sure that the clip or coupling is in good condition and is not bent, cracked or rusted. A faulty connection here will make the linkage liable to failure — in view of the time you have spent removing the trim, it's well worth fitting a new clip or coupling if you have any doubts about its condition.

Whether the linkage is made of a circular rod or a flat steel bar, you should also check that is not bent out of its original shape. Sometimes, either through rough handling or from getting in the way of the window regulator, the rod can become distorted so that it does not pull the lever on the catch mechanism far enough to open the door. Before bending the rod back to its original shape, you should have a look at the linkage on the other door to get an idea of the correct shape. Only bend the rod a little at a time until it clears all obstructions and is extended far enough to operate the catch mechanism fully.

Before replacing the inner trim, check the operation of the mechanism carefully. This involves temporarily refitting the inner door handle and opening and closing the door from inside the car. You should also lightly oil the catch mechanism by reaching inside the door with a small oil can, then smear petroleum jelly over the ends of the linkages. Once you are sure that everything is

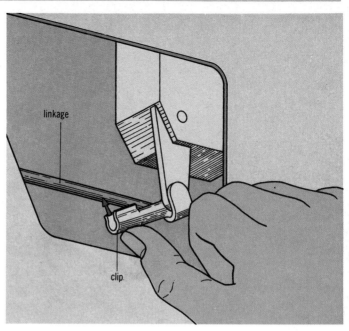

3. Clipping the rod firmly into place

working correctly refit the interior trim. When the trim is back in place, check again that

everything is working smoothly without catching on the trim panel.

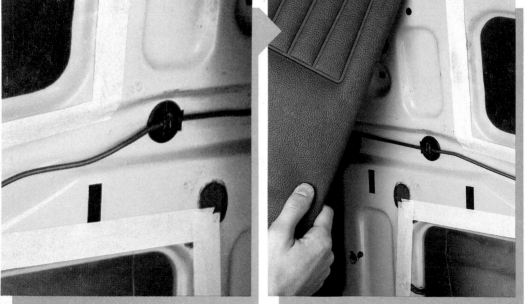

4. This linkage has become damaged

5. Check other side of car for correct shape

Usually the inside locking buttons are trouble free, although on some cars with push button locks the plastic stem can split so that the button snaps off. These are cheap and simple to replace — they simply screw on to the threaded end of the rod which protrudes through the top of the door.

If the button is in place, but does not make the door lock, there is probably a problem with the linkage rod which runs straight down to the catch mechanism. Either the rod has become bent or its end has become detached from the lever on the catch — see Step 3. Your locking mechanism will probably be designed in such a way that the button will not go up or down unless the car door is closed. Wind down the window so that you can work the locking button from the inside and then reach outside to operate the door handle.

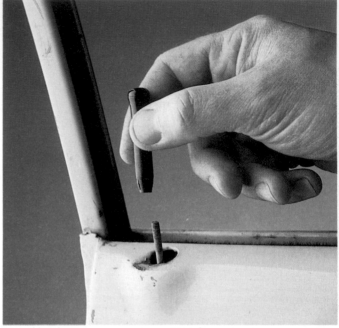

1. Locking button may screw on to rod

TIP

By hook or by crook

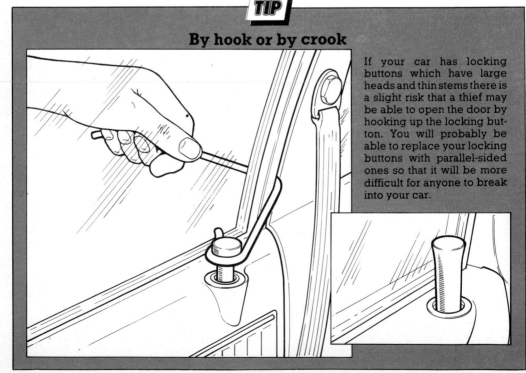

If your car has locking buttons which have large heads and thin stems there is a slight risk that a thief may be able to open the door by hooking up the locking button. You will probably be able to replace your locking buttons with parallel-sided ones so that it will be more difficult for anyone to break into your car.

If the doors still fail to open or close reliably and you are confident that the door catch and striker plate are properly aligned and tightened, it may be that the striker mechanism itself is faulty. This could be caused by wear, but it is more likely that the mechanism has become corroded. Removing the old mechanism and fitting a new one is a fairly straightforward job on most cars. After you have removed the interior trim, reach inside the door and disconnect all the linkages which are attached to the mechanism (**fig 1**). Now look at the side of the door around the catch and you will see three or four large crosshead screws which hold the mechanism in place. Often these are very tight and can only be loosened by using a tee-handled screwdriver or an impact tool. With the screws removed, the mechanism can be lifted away from inside the door. Fitting a new one is a reversal of this procedure, but make sure you tighten the screws fully. You may have to readjust the striker plate to allow for the new catch. Fit a new striker plate as well if the old one is badly worn.

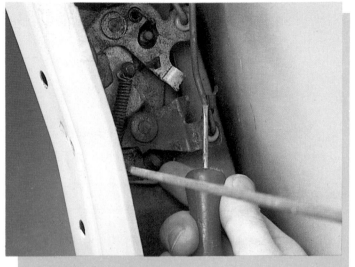

1. Releasing clip which holds rod in place

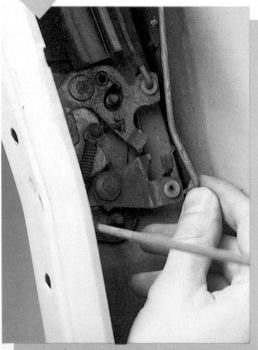

2. Pulling linkage rod from hole in catch

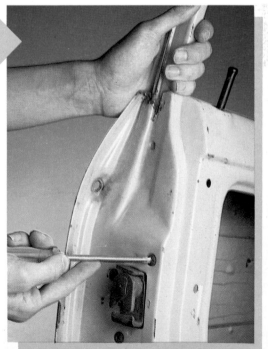

3. Unfastening catch from door frame

If your lock has failed completely or your key has broken off inside the lock and cannot be retrieved the only alternative is to renew the lock.

On some cars with the lock incorporated in the door handle, this can mean replacing the entire unit. On other cars — including many Ford models — it is possible just to buy the lock barrel and fit it to the original handle. On cars where the lock is separate from the handle, the job simply involves removing the panel trim, disconnecting the linkage from the inside of the lock and undoing the clip, bolts or nuts which hold the lock to the door (**fig 1**).

On cars where the lock is built into the door handle, you will have to remove the whole assembly (see Step 2).

If your dealer tells you that he can supply the lock barrels separate from the whole handle assembly, you may find that this is a job you can do yourself. Often the hardest part is removing the handle and once this is out of the car all you have to do is remove either a clip, a pin or a bolt which holds the barrel in the handle assembly so that the new barrel can be fitted. Some manufacturers, like Citroën, supply the barrels only as a set of three so that the locks in both the front doors and boot will all accept the same key.

If this is the case, you will find

1. Lock is fastened to the inside of door frame

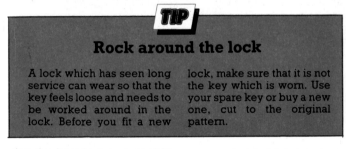

TIP

Rock around the lock

A lock which has seen long service can wear so that the key feels loose and needs to be worked around in the lock. Before you fit a new lock, make sure that it is not the key which is worn. Use your spare key or buy a new one, cut to the original pattern.

that the boot lock is probably very easy to replace — mainly because it is usually so much more easily reached. The lock assembly must first be unscrewed or unbolted from inside the boot lid (**fig 3**). Once the lock assembly has been lifted away, the barrel can be removed by either prising away its retaining clip or undoing the screws that hold it in place. Slide the new barrel back in its place and secure it.

If you buy a lock separately, however, you will have to put up with the inconvenience of having two different keys for the front doors. In other cases — such as the BL Mini — the lock and handle assembly have to be purchased as a single unit.

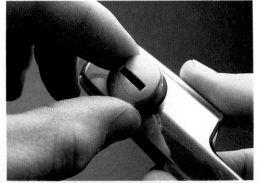

2. Key barrel may be separate assembly

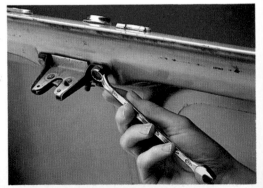

3. Removing bolts which hold boot lock

How to repair dents and chips

Don't be afraid of bodywork repairs. If you prepare well and choose the correct materials, you can achieve a great result

Careful preparation is the key to success in bodywork repairs. This includes removing all the paint and rust in the affected area, rustproofing, applying filler and primer.

That said, the faster you do the job, the better. This is because you are sure to get areas of exposed metal at some stage of the job. So cover them quickly to stop rust setting in.

When to do this job
When you have chips, stone bruises and dents not more than about ½ in. (12 mm) deep and a handspan wide

What this job involves
Preparing the surface
Removing any rust
Filling chip(s) or dent(s)
Priming

Points to watch
Do not use ordinary abrasive paper on your car bodywork as it will leave bits all over the surface and it will be hard to get a good finish. Use production paper for coarse work followed by wet and dry for smoothing down

To do this job
Tools: Wire brush; rasp or Surform; electric drill with grinding attachment (maybe); small artist's-type paintbrush
Materials: Wet-and-dry abrasive paper in grades 200, 400 and 600; rustproofing compound; cellulose putty; epoxy resin filler (dents only); white spirit; zinc-based primer
Time: About 2 hours, spread over two or three days
Degree of difficulty: No experience needed, but requires great care and patience

If you have this job professionally done . . .
Is the repaired area invisible against its surrounding metal? Does new colour match exactly?

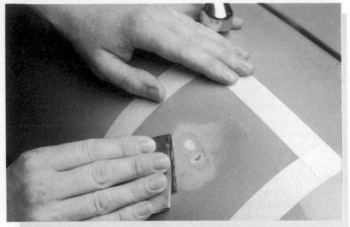

1. Rubbing away paint with wet-and-dry until metal gleams

2. Scoring with wire brush

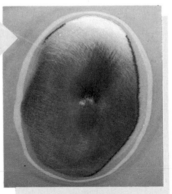

3. Ready for filling

Before you begin any repair, use a good car shampoo to make sure the area is clean.

Next, apply short strips of masking tape in a tight square around the repair area. This will protect the surrounding paint-work from accidental scratches.

What you do next depends on the type of repair needed:

Dents which have not broken the paint surface

Rub away the paint with coarse grade wet-and-dry (see Fact File box) until the metal below gleams, covering an area a little larger than the dent (**fig 1**). This step is essential — if you simply apply filler straight on to the paintwork it may lift off.

Then use a wire brush, a sharp knife or a sheet of coarse wet-and-dry to score the metal surface (**fig 2**). This will provide a good key for the filler (**fig 3**).

Now proceed to Step 2.

Chips which have not exposed bare metal

Smooth the edges of the old paintwork with 400 grade wet-and-dry, used wet. This will lightly score the bottom of the

TIP

Time saver

Removing the paint from an area of bodywork can be a tedious chore — particularly with the larger dents. You can make the job easier with a flap wheel attachment on an electric drill.

Use a coarse grade of flap for this job — the finer ones are more suited to smoothing down.

A flap wheel is easier to control on paintwork than a wire brush is — but a wire brush works better on rust.

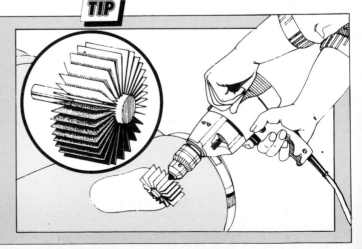

chip — enough to hold a fine layer of filler — but do not make the chip any deeper than you can help.

Now go to Alternative Step 3.

Dents or chips which have exposed bare metal

If you can see any rust, you can be almost certain that it will have taken hold not just where the chip or dent is, but also in the area immediately around it.

So use the point of a penknife to pick away the paint until all the rust is exposed and you reach clean metal.

(If the rust is very even-looking, and you do not seem to reach clean metal even if you are an inch (25 mm) or so out from the dent, stop work. You may be unlucky enough to have a panel which was not painted properly in the first place, and which has a fine coating of rust all over. Short of stripping and respraying the whole panel,

about the only thing you can do is fill the immediate hole.)

Now remove all traces of paint and rust from the area to be repaired. If the rust has bitten very deep, you may find that you need a wire brush, or even an electric drill with a small conical grinding attachment. These grinders are widely available from car accessory shops or model shops, but a piece of tightly-folded 200 grade wet-and-dry will do almost as good a job.

Using wet-and-dry

The best type of abrasive paper for car bodywork repairs is wet-and-dry — so called because it can be used either wet or dry. Used dry, it is more abrasive at first but rapidly clogs with particles of paint. Used wet, it is initially less abrasive but clogs far less rapidly and can be rinsed clean when it does. It is best used with cold water — though reasonably waterproof, warm or soapy water will shorten its life.

Wet-and-dry is available in a

wide variety of grades. These are numbered according to their roughness — the lower the number the coarser the paper. For car repairs you will find the most useful grades are 200, 400 and 600. Lower, rougher grades might appear to do the job faster but they will often remove too much material or badly scratch the surrounding paintwork.

It is a good idea to keep well-used sheets for the later stages of a repair.

STEP 2   REMOVE ANY RUST

1. Applying a coat of rustproofer with small paintbrush

Once you have the metal clean and bright, rust will start to form immediately, though it does not become obvious at first. So brush on a coat of chemical rust remover such as Jenolite or Trustan 400 (**fig 1**).

This will effectively neutralize any surface corrosion (though not rust that has penetrated right through) and inhibit further rusting.

Take great care not to spill the rustproofer on your skin or on the car's paintwork.

Most rust removers are acid based and are simply brushed on, left to react and then washed off with clean water. As soon as the area is dry start filling the dent or chip.

For repairing dents, start with an epoxy resin filler such as P38 or Plastic Padding. This is a two-pack filler, comprising a paste and a hardener that have to be mixed, which sets hard and can be sanded to a smooth surface.

Once mixed, epoxy resin filler hardens in about 20 minutes. This time can be increased or decreased by varying the amount of hardener you use. For most applications a 1:10 hardener-to-paste mixture is about right, but the exact proportions are not critical. Make sure the filler is thoroughly mixed to a consistent colour.

It is impossible to get body filler to follow exactly the original contours of the car. However careful you are, you will always have to overfill and then sand back. But the more you overfill, the more sanding you will have to do.

So build up the filler layer by layer, about ¼ in. (6 mm) at a time. Do this by using a flexible spatula to press the filler firmly into the dent (**figs 4 & 5**). Leave the top surface of each layer rough to provide a 'key' for the next layer.

Wait until each layer has stopped being sticky — but not until it is rock-hard — before applying the next layer.

Once your top layer is standing slightly proud of the surface, wait for it to set. Then start sanding down. First, remove any obvious ridges or high spots with a file, rasp or a Surform. This is better than coarse sandpaper, which might slip and score the surrounding paintwork.

As the filler gets closer to its final shape, swap first to 400 grade wet-and-dry (used wet) and then to 600 grade (also used wet) (**fig 6**). It is best to wrap the sandpaper around a cork block or small piece of wood so you can control it better — if you use just your fingers you will probably wear hollows in the middle of the repaired area.

When you have finished

1. Mix filler and hardener in correct proportions

2. Use a spatula to mix thoroughly

3. Final colour must be even, not streaked

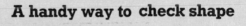

TIP

A handy way to check shape

A woodworker's profile gauge comes in handy when sanding down a filled dent. Carefully set its points to match an undamaged area, then scrape it over the filled dent. It will score any filler standing proud.

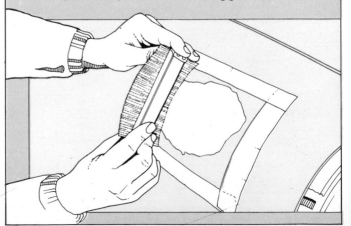

sanding, the filler should be just a coat of paint lower than the surrounding area. This is very hard to judge by eye. So — depending on which bit of the car you are working on — use a steel rule, or a bit of cardboard cut to match the curve of the car, or both, to help you.

You are almost certain to end up with a number of tiny flaws in the surface of the filler, so give the filled area a thin coat of cellulose stopper. Rub the stopper down with wet and dry.

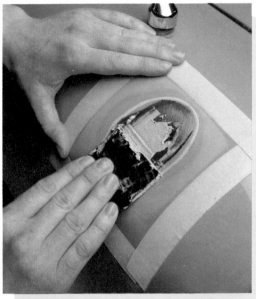

4. Applying initial thin layer of filler

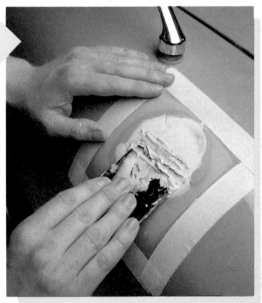

5. Building up the filler layer by layer

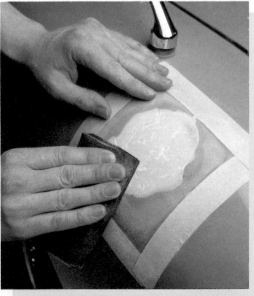

6. Sanding rough spots with wet-and-dry

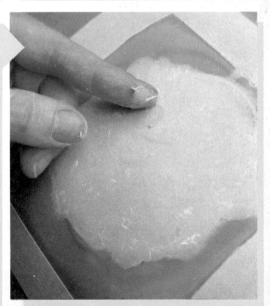

7. Filling tiny flaws using a fingertip

15

Body repairs with glassfibre

Rust holes in car bodywork look ugly, but it's easy to get a professional looking repair if you use glassfibre to fix them

Glassfibre is ideal for repairing rust holes in car bodywork. When wet it is pliable, and moulds easily to the shape of a hole and the contour of the panel, and it can be worked into awkward corners to fill holes.

When it dries, glassfibre is very strong, waterproof and rotproof and can be filled, sanded and sprayed like any other repair. With care it can even be drilled to take fittings like mirrors and trim.

When working with glassfibre make sure you have plenty of ventilation and take care not to smoke nearby as it is highly flammable.

You can buy glassfibre in kits which usually include the resin, hardener and mat, but if you need surfacing tissue you have to buy it separately. Different sizes of kit are also available.

Glassfibre should only be

When to do this job
When you have a rust hole or large gash in a panel

What this job involves
Cutting out rusty metal
Using aluminium or zinc mesh
Using glassfibre mat

Points to watch
Cut the glassfibre cloth with an old pair of scissors or a very sharp knife
Apply the resin with an old paint brush or a cheap one bought for the purpose

To do this job
Tools: Hammer; metal cutter; paintbrush; mixing dish
Materials: Glassfibre mat; finishing mat (maybe); resin; hardener; filler; aluminium or zinc mesh; rust preventer; wet-and-dry paper
Time: Several hours depending on size of repair
Degree of difficulty: Easy on flat, easy-to-reach panels. Care needed when handling resin and hardener

If you have the job professionally done . . .
Is the repair properly finished? Has underseal been applied to the underside of the repair (if applicable)?

used for repairing panels that are not part of the main structure of the car and do not act as load bearing areas.

Repairs to the door sills, underbody crossmembers, seat belt mountings and seat mounting points, for example can only be done with welding equipment. If you try to use glassfibre not only will the car fail the MoT roadworthiness test but it will be unsafe.

The sort of panels you can repair with glassfibre are doors, wings, bonnets, bootlids and some rear panels. Remember that although glassfibre is very strong it will not stand up to a sudden impact nor offer the same protection as steel.

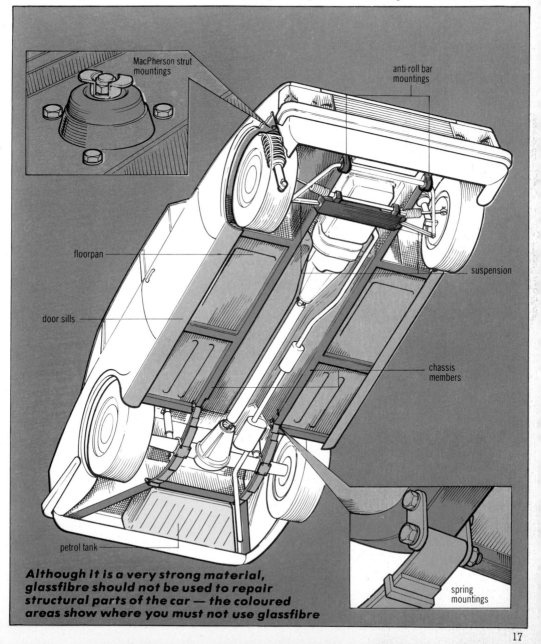

MacPherson strut mountings

anti-roll bar mountings

floorpan

suspension

door sills

chassis members

petrol tank

spring mountings

Although it is a very strong material, glassfibre should not be used to repair structural parts of the car — the coloured areas show where you must not use glassfibre

Before you try to repair a rusty or damaged area with glass-fibre the paintwork around it must be stripped down to bare metal to find the exact extent of the damage. It is pointless to try to apply glassfibre on top of rusty metal — the repair will soon crack or lift off and the job will have to be done again.

Use coarse production paper, or a very coarse sanding disc that you can get from a body specialist to remove the paint and any rust from the area. Start from the centre of the rusted spot and work outwards. Keep sanding until you reveal a fringe of rust-free metal all round the rusty area (**fig 1**).

Quite often the area of paint-work you have to strip will be much larger than you first thought. This will reveal either a surface covered in small rust holes or a large rust hole — or the full extent of a gash.

If you can get behind the panel you are working on, you should remove all traces of dirt and corrosion from this too. If the panel is undersealed remove this first by scraping off

Using glassfibre

Glassfibre matting and surfacing tissue
Glassfibre matting is a versatile material which, when impregnated with a resin, sets hard. Mat can be used to strengthen and reinforce existing panels or can be moulded to shape to make completely new ones. You can also use it to help blend new panels like spoilers or wheel arch extensions into the existing bodywork.

Glassfibre matting comes in three grades — coarse, medium and fine tissue. The first two are made of rather coarse fibres which remain visible through the resin coat, even after spray painting. As such these mats are more suitable for repairs which will not be seen — like the underside of panels.

Surfacing tissue is very fine and can be used to build up a fine smooth surface. This type is useful for the outside of body-work panels. Surfacing tissue is usually used along with two-part epoxy filler which, along with the matting, can be rubbed down to give a perfectly smooth surface suitable for spraying.

Resin and hardener
Resin will not set glassfibre matting until a hardening agent is added to it. When resin and hardener are mixed together a chemical reaction takes place — and once it has started the resin sets hard in about 20 or 30 minutes, so if you have a very large repair to do it is best to only mix enough for a small section at one time.

The resin and hardener can be mixed in an old plastic tub or a clean tin can — do not use a container which might get used for food preparation. Tip the resin in first then add the hardener. This will be either in tube form as a coloured paste, or a colourless liquid in a bottle — whichever sort you have the procedure is the same.

Make sure you use the amount recommended by the instructions — it is a waste to use too much as the resin will not dry any quicker. If you use too little the drying time will not be lengthened by more than a few minutes and the chances are that the resin will not dry at all and you will have to remove the whole sticky mess and start the job again.

If you want to be able to control the drying time of your resin then choose one of the one-part types which only harden when exposed to daylight. To stop it drying all you have to do is cover it with a black cloth or plastic bag.

Stir the hardener into the resin with a strong plastic spoon or a piece of scrap wood. Keep on mixing until you are certain that all the hardener is mixed, otherwise some parts of the repair may not harden. Once you have done this you are ready to apply it to the repair.

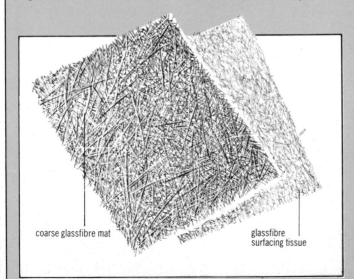

coarse glassfibre mat

glassfibre surfacing tissue

1. Sanding the rusted area to reveal the full extent of damage

the hard outer skin. Then use a rag dampened with petrol to remove the traces. Finally wash the panel and dry it thoroughly — this should leave a good surface which the glassfibre and resin or filler will firmly adhere to.

The approach to each repair is quite different so follow the step which deals with the type of damage you have.

Remember that you are using chemicals when you mix the resin and hardener so take some precautions. Be especially careful not to get neat hardener on your skin. It contains chemicals which will give you a nasty rash. Wear a pair of rubber gloves to protect your hands — if you do accidentally spill any on yourself then wash the affected area with lots of clean water. If any goes in your eyes or mouth wash the area with clean water and see a doctor straight away.

Techniques for glassfibre repairs
Glassfibre resin has to be stippled into the mat with a paint-brush (below). Stippling means dabbing the end of the brush gently into the mat — it is the only method which will work the

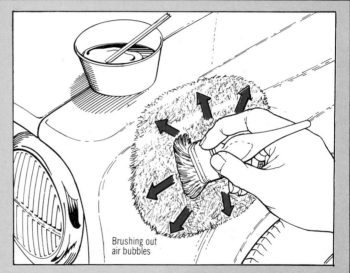

Brushing out air bubbles

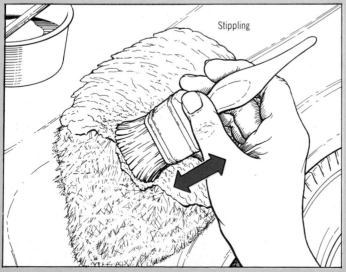

Stippling

resin right in. Do not dab too hard, and keep the brush wet with resin or the mat may stick to it and wrinkle.

Keep dabbing resin on until the mat is thoroughly saturated, but make sure it does not stand proud of the rest of the panel.

Try not to brush the resin on to the mat — it will not soak in and you may pull the mat off the panel. Any air bubbles under the mat have to be removed before it dries or the glassfibre will be weakened. To do this you must lightly brush the surface of the mat — work from the centre outwards (above), keeping the brush wet with resin, until all the bubbles have gone and allow the repair to dry.

Finally, use a thin coat of filler to disguise the repair and blend it smoothly into the rest of the panel.

1. A panel with pinhole rusting

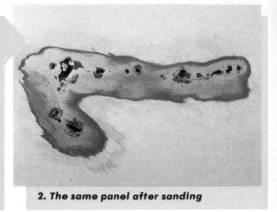

2. The same panel after sanding

Small holes, especially rust pinholes can be repaired from the back or front of a panel, depending on how easy it is to get at the back of the panel. Repairs made from behind normally give a neater finish even though the job is more involved, so try to use this method if possible. If not see Alternative Step 2.

First clean all the dirt, underseal and rust from the surrounding area (see Step 1) and paint on several coats of rust inhibitor. You will need at least two sheets of glassfibre mat to ensure a good, strong repair — cut the mat so that it overlaps the edge of the damaged area by about ½ in. (13 mm) all round.

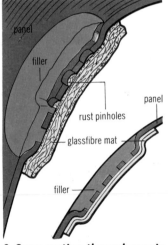

3. Cross-section through repair

(labels: panel, filler, rust pinholes, panel, glassfibre mat, filler)

Mix up the resin and hardener (see Fact File) and brush a layer on to the back of the panel being careful not to drip any on yourself. Press the mat carefully into place making sure it sticks to the metal (**fig 4**). Using the paintbrush saturate the mat with a gentle stippling action — dabbing the end of the brush carefully out on to the mat — so that the mat is thoroughly impregnated, and then leave it to dry. Brush on more resin and stick the second sheet into position. Once this has dried you can fill the dent with resin filler from the front. Keep water out of the back of the repair with a coat of paint followed by a coat of underseal.

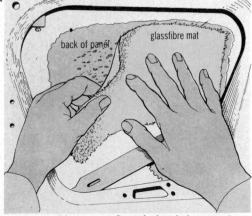

(labels: back of panel, glassfibre mat)

4. Laying the mat on from behind the panel

5. Applying a layer of filler to the repair

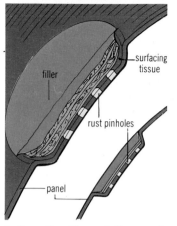

1. A section through the repair

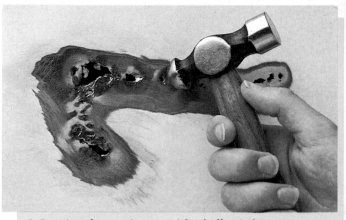

2. Denting the repair area with a ball-pein hammer

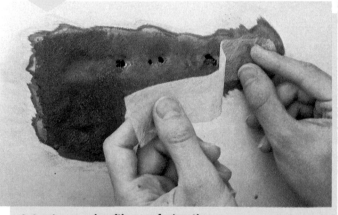

3. Laying on glassfibre surfacing tissue

4. Feathering the repair into the rest of the panel

Repairing a perforated area from the front is very much simpler than from behind. Strip the repair down to bare metal as described in Step 1 then brush on a rust inhibitor. Now use a ball-pein hammer to dent the panel in about ¼ in. (7 mm) below the general level (**fig 2**).

To make filling easier use glassfibre surfacing tissue (see Fact File) — this is much finer than ordinary mat and will help you get a smooth surface when rubbing down at a later stage.

Cut two sheets of surfacing tissue bigger all round by about ½ in. (13 mm) than the holed area. Apply the resin and hardener mix to the front of the panel and press the first piece of mat firmly into place (**fig 3**), making sure it is stuck all round. Again, stipple more resin in and leave the repair to dry. Check that the mat is not standing proud of the surrounding surface. If it is then sand it back to bare metal and dent the panel down further. Then apply another sheet as before.

Once you have put two sheets of mat on the repair and both have dried, sand the repair (**fig 4**) and use epoxy resin filler to restore the shape of the body panel.

Clean the resin out of your brush with cellulose thinners.

To make a good repair to largish rust holes all the rusty metal has to be cut out, otherwise the glassfibre will not take to the panel or rust will again break out around the repaired area.

First find out how far the rust has spread by rubbing down the paintwork around the damaged area as shown in Step 1. Now decide how much metal around the holes needs to be removed to ensure no traces are left — this varies but, generally, cutting about ½ in. (13 mm) into clean metal should be enough. It is easiest to use tin snips with cranked handles to cut away the metal around the hole (**fig 1**) — these also give the neatest results. But if you cannot get hold of any, a hacksaw blade will do the job (see Tip — Hole cutter).

Whatever method you use, do not try to follow the contour of the rust hole too closely — it is easier to cut glassfibre mat to fit

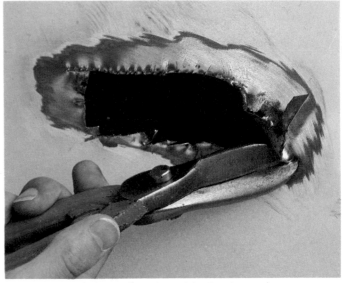

1. Cutting out the rusted section with tin snips

a four-sided hole, and you run the risk of damaging the panel if you try to cut out a sharply

curved shape around the edge of the rusted area.

Once the rust has been cut out sand the area around the hole back to bare metal to give the glassfibre a clean surface to bond on to. Then tap the edges of the repair down about ¼ in. (7 mm) all around the hole with a ball-pein hammer. This allows the repair materials to be recessed and prevents ugly bulges on the panel surface. You can now start to repair the rust hole. Try to do this from the back. If you cannot do this, make the repair as shown in Alternative Step 3.

Next, cut four pieces of glass-fibre mat each of which overlap the edges of the hole by about 2 in. (50 mm).

Using masking tape stick a piece of card (see Tip — Non-stick support) into position over the hole on the outside of the panel (**fig 3**). Try to get it to follow the contour of the panel — this will avoid too much filling later on.

The secret of using glassfibre to repair holes is not to try and put too many layers on in one go. If you do, the repair will sag,

TIP

Hole cutter

If you do not have a pair of tinsnips you can cut out the rust with a hacksaw blade. Wrap a thick wad of cloth round the end of the blade to protect your hand.

Cut a series of slots outwards from the rust hole

until it reaches good metal. If the metal is thin you may be able to break off the metal stub by bending it backwards and forwards — otherwise you will have to use pliers to bend the stub up and the blade to cut it off.

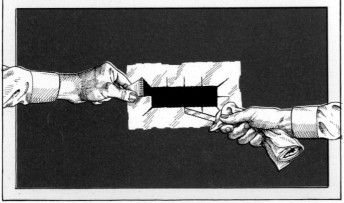

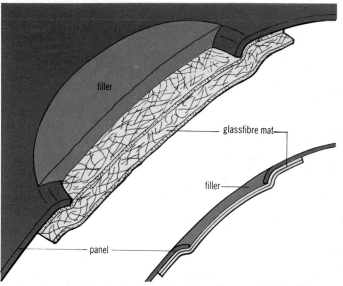

filler

glassfibre mat

filler

panel

2. A section (top) and cutaway show how the repair is built up

Non-stick support

To support the glassfibre while it dries and to shape it roughly to the contour of the panel you are repairing, try this simple dodge.

Cut a piece of cardboard about ½ in. (13 mm) bigger all round than the hole. Cover the card in a sheet of plain coloured thick polythene (a strong plastic bag will do).

Tape it over the front of the hole with masking tape. The glassfibre will stick to it as it dries, and you can then peel off the card to leave a smooth surface which is ready for filling with epoxy filler to complete the repair.

and air bubbles will be trapped in the repair and weaken it.

Brush some of the resin mix on to the metal around the back of the hole. Press the first piece of glassfibre mat into place, making sure that it sticks to the resin around the edge of the hole. Stipple more resin into the mat until it is saturated.

Try to avoid brushing the resin into the mat, as it can move the mat away from the hole. When you are sure that the mat is saturated with resin gently brush the repair to get rid of any air bubbles which are trapped between the repair and the panel (see Fact File).

Leave the repair to harden for about half an hour (or until it is touch dry) and then repeat the job again, remembering to brush out any air bubbles from each layer. Once the final layer has dried properly you can carefully remove the card-board from the front and lightly sand the surface with 400 grade wet-and-dry paper.

Finish the repair by applying body filler over the glassfibre mat from the front, rubbing it down flush with the surrounding

contours of the metal.

As glassfibre is easily cracked by a sharp impact it is a good idea to coat the underside

of the repair with underseal to protect it from stones thrown up by the wheels. Do not forget to clean your brush out.

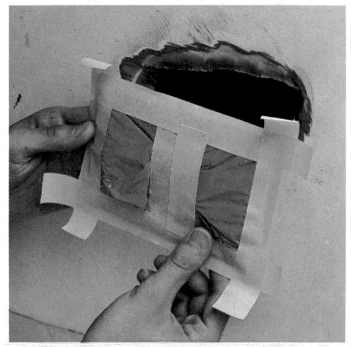

3. Sticking polythene and card support over the hole

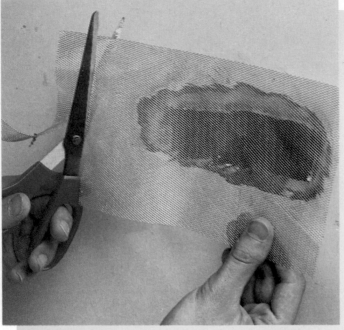

1. Cutting the aluminium mesh to size

Double-skinned panels, like some rear wings or rear panels, cannot be repaired from behind, so the only solution is to make the repair from the front.

First cut out the rust and prepare the area (see Steps 1 and 3). The glassfibre needs to be supported while it is drying and the best material to use is expanded aluminium or zinc mesh. This can be bent and cut to fit behind the hole and will hold the mat securely in position until it has set.

Cut a piece of mesh about 1 in. (25 mm) bigger all round than the hole (**fig 1**), and push a loop of wire through the centre of the mesh. Now mix up a small quantity of resin filler and apply it in small blobs to the edges of the mesh (**fig 2**). Holding the ends of the wire loop, carefully ease the mesh through the rust hole and then draw it up so that it sticks to the back of the panel. Hold the mesh in place with the wire loop

2. Applying filler to edges of the mesh

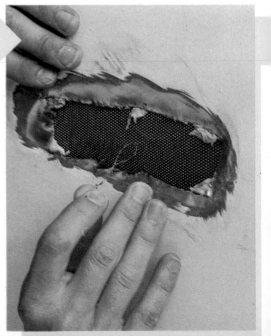

3. Holding the mesh while filler dries

until the filler is dry (**fig 3**) — only take out the wire when you are sure the filler has dried.

Make a cardboard template the same shape and size as the hole and use this to cut out three pieces of glassfibre mat — make the first piece a little larger than the template, the second slightly larger, and so on. Your third sheet should overlap the hole by ½ in. (13 mm) all round. For a better finish cut the third sheet out of glassfibre surfacing tissue. This will leave a smoother, more easily sanded repair than ordinary mat.

Next, mix enough resin and hardener (see Fact File) for the repair. It is better to mix too much rather than too little — if you run out of resin half way through the stippling you will have to mix up more and the resin you applied earlier may have begun to cure.

Brush a coating of resin on to the mesh and the edges of the repair. Lay the first sheet of

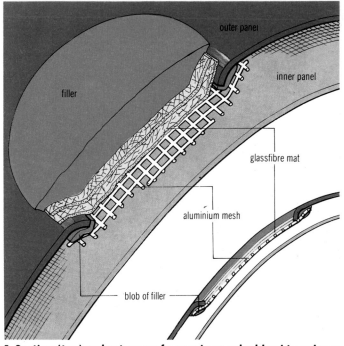

5. Section (top) and cutaway of a repair on a double-skinned panel

outer panel

inner panel

filler

glassfibre mat

aluminium mesh

blob of filler

4. Stippling resin into the surfacing tissue

glassfibre into place and stipple it with plenty of resin. Leave it to dry and then put the second piece of mat on — make sure it overlaps the first one but does not stand proud of the bodywork.

Check that you can put on the third layer without causing it to stand above the level of the surrounding area. If you can, then leave the glassfibre to dry and use filler to bring the repair flush with the panel surface in the normal way.

If there is room for another layer on top of the first three, use surfacing tissue (**fig 4**) to bring the level up. Leave the repair to harden and then rub it down with medium (400) grade wet-and-dry paper to key the surface for the filler.

Apply a layer of filler and sand it down until it is flush with the rest of the panel.

Finally, clean your brush thoroughly in cellulose thinners.

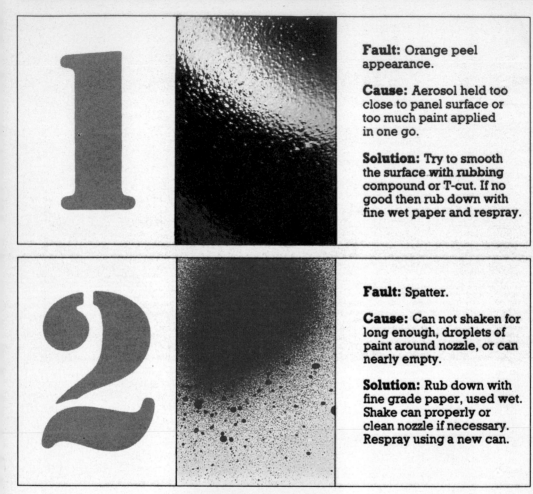

Fault: Orange peel appearance.

Cause: Aerosol held too close to panel surface or too much paint applied in one go.

Solution: Try to smooth the surface with rubbing compound or T-cut. If no good then rub down with fine wet paper and respray.

Fault: Spatter.

Cause: Can not shaken for long enough, droplets of paint around nozzle, or can nearly empty.

Solution: Rub down with fine grade paper, used wet. Shake can properly or clean nozzle if necessary. Respray using a new can.

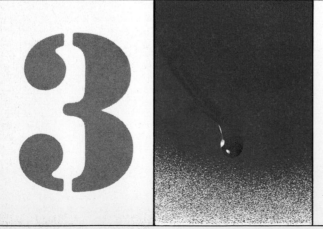

Fault: Runs or sags.

Cause: Too much paint applied in one application.

Solution: Wait until the paint is thoroughly dry. Rub down with fine grade abrasive paper used wet, and respray.

A rosol painting —the right way

Aerosol spray paints offer a convenient, relatively cheap and easy way to paint body panels up to the size of a wing

With care and practice you can get a finish very close to the factory original. Take plenty of time — the finished result will reflect the amount of care and effort you put in.

When to do this job
After filling dents and holes in the bodywork
After repairing any area of bodywork which is too large to be brush painted with touch-up paint
After fitting new panels or parts

What this job involves
Cleaning and masking a bodywork repair
Spraying and rubbing down primer paint
Filling small imperfections in the primer coat
Spraying topcoat
Finishing techniques

Points to watch
Car colours are very difficult to match. If you cannot find the exact colour, take along the petrol cap or a similar part as a sample
Buy big aerosols rather than little ones as they give much better results

To do this job
Tools: Plastic spatula (see text)
Materials: Aerosol primer paint; aerosol topcoat paint; cellulose thinners; wet-and-dry paper (400, 600, 800, 1200 grades); cellulose putty; masking tape; newspaper; clean rags; rubbing/cutting compound (maybe)
Time: Three hours, spread over two or three days
Degree of difficulty: Needs practice with an aerosol to get a good finish

If you have the job professionally done . . .
Is the newly sprayed panel the same colour and smoothness as the rest of the car? Is there any paint overspray on bumpers, lights or body panels?

To avoid spraying over parts you do not want painted and to cut down the amount of masking you have to do, or to improve accessibility to a panel, you may have to remove pieces of trim and components on or close to the spray area. This also leads to a more professional looking finish when the job is complete.

Parts such as bumpers, number plates, mirrors and screen wipers can be simply unbolted or unscrewed where possible (**figs 1-4**). But door trim, body strips and name badges are slightly less straightforward to remove.

Car manufacturers use a variety of different clips and

fittings to secure badges and door side trim. The most common types of clip and how to remove the trim are shown in the Fact File — Trim and badge fixings.

If the fittings come off easily then remove them. If not, leave them in place and mask them carefully (see Step 2).

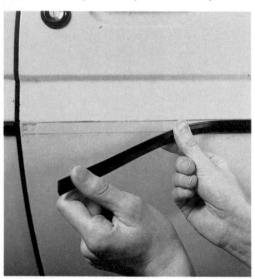

1. Pulling off the side trim

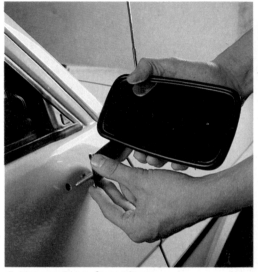

2. Unscrewing a door mirror

3. Removing the aerial

4. Taking off the wipers

Trim and badge fixings

Body side trim strips and name badges are fixed to bodywork in a variety of ways and may need to be removed for bodywork repairs, or when damaged.

Strip trim is usually a tight push fit over clips which are attached to the body. These clips may be plastic or metal and are usually quite flimsy, so take care when removing trim. Trim usually has to be prised off metal clips (use a flat piece of wood so that you do not damage the paintwork), or slid off plastic clips, working from one end of the strip. If you cannot discover what type of clips you have without removing the trim, prise off a short length at one end and be prepared for a breakage — the clips are inexpensive and simply push on to or screw into the bodywork.

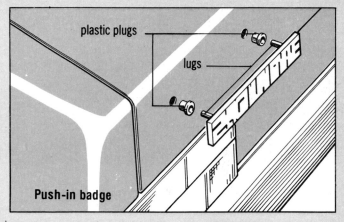

plastic plugs

lugs

Push-in badge

Name, marque or model badges are usually a push fit into holes in the bodywork or held by pull-off clips. Lever off the latter with a screwdriver if the back of the panel is accessible, or carefully prise away the push-fit type from the front.

Some cars, particularly newer models, have badges fixed to bodywork with glue or powerful adhesive backing. Test for this by carefully trying to prise the badge away. If it shows no sign of moving, leave it in place rather than risk damage to paint and bodywork. If a stick-on badge does come off, clean all traces of glue off the paintwork with lighter fuel. When you come to stick the badge back on, check that the glue you use will not react with the paintwork. If necessary test it on a small area which does not show, such as inside the boot.

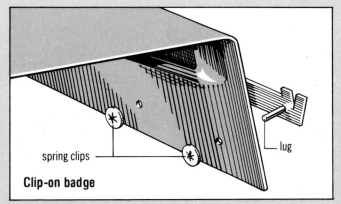

spring clips

lug

Clip-on badge

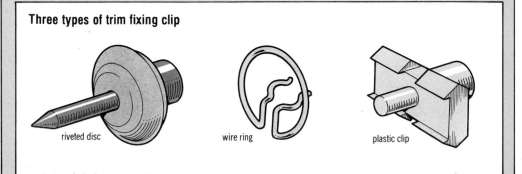

Three types of trim fixing clip

riveted disc

wire ring

plastic clip

1. Masking exposed components

Masking is essential to prevent paint from going anywhere but on the part you want to spray. Masking tape, available from most accessory stores, is used for this. Do not use other sticky tapes as substitutes — most tend to wrinkle when sprayed, allowing paint to creep underneath. They may even pull off newly sprayed paint when you try to remove them, or leave hard-to-remove deposits.

Small components in the spray area can be completely covered with masking tape (**fig 1**). Larger areas, like windscreens or adjoining panels, should be covered with newspaper. Seal down the newspaper with masking tape along its edges, and also where sheets of newspaper overlap.

Where possible, make use of natural lines to follow when masking — like the waist or sill lines, bonnet edges or panel edges. This makes positioning the tape easier, particularly on longer tape runs. It also helps to

Before spraying on bodywork, spend a short time practising your technique. A vertical surface is easiest to begin with — practise on scrap metal, hardboard or even shiny, non-absorbent paper. (Wood is not much use — it is far too absorbent.) Better still, respray your wheels; mistakes will not be too obvious and the many facets and shapes of wheel hubs will provide good practice in spraying as well as masking.

Start by following instructions on the spray can — shake the can as recommended to ensure the paint is properly mixed.

Next, hold the can upright, at right angles to the surface, and make a false pass along the top of the practice panel. Whether this is contoured, curved or flat, keep the spray nozzle a consistent 8 in. (200 mm) away as you move from edge to edge (**fig 1**).

Now make a 'real' pass over your practice panel. Depress the nozzle button fully before reaching the panel edge and make an even sweep from side to side. Do not pivot the can from you wrist — this results in a more concentrated film of paint in the middle than at the edges of the work (**fig 2**). Try to move your

whole arm across evenly and do not stop moving or release the button part way across. Release the spray button only after you have sprayed past the far edge of your work.

Now move down the panel, spraying in even bands from top to bottom. Do not try for perfect coverage in one coat. Applying one thick coat will cause the paint to run and sag leaving an unsightly mess that must be painstakingly rubbed flat.

Colour matching

Providing your car has not been resprayed with a non-original colour, the best way to make sure you buy exactly the right colour paint is to check your car's colour identification plate. The plate's position should be given in your car's handbook but the illustration shows the most common locations.

If you think that your car may have been resprayed, check door sills and the floor pan for colour match. If the new colour is a special mix you will either have to try to find the best off-the-shelf colour match or find a paint shop that will mix your colour for you.

Colour matching the paint on a new or newly resprayed car is usually quite straightforward — older cars can be problematical. In time some paints fade while others oxidize and darken.

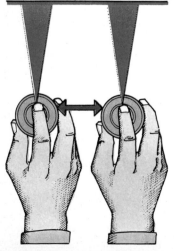
1. Move your arm not the can

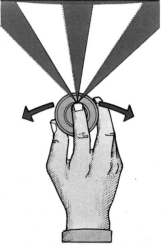
2. Try not to swing the can

disguise the joint between old paint and new.

If you have to mask over a raised area or component, make sure the tape does not overlap on to surrounding paintwork. If possible try to push or tuck tape under fixed trim, such as rubber seals, with the blunt side of a knife blade.

Finally, when you are happy with the positioning of the tape, run the ball of a spoon over all the inside edges to ensure it is firmly stuck down.

Clean seals

TIP

Many spray jobs are spoilt by traces of overspray on the rubber seals, or by a telltale ridge of paint that builds up in front of the masking. You can overcome this by raising the lip of a seal using the handle of a spoon, and pushing a length of string under it. Mask the seal and spray — the paint will go under the seal, not on top.

3. How to spray a flat panel

You get a better finish if you spray several thin coats, allowing the manufacturer's drying time between coats. Spraying on a still tacky coat may cause the paint to crack or craze and you will have to start from scratch.

When you come to spray horizontal panels, like the car roof, boot or bonnet, rather than upright ones, like doors and side panels, you will encounter different problems. To make the best job on these you must be able to look down on the panel. Stand on a step ladder or wooden box to give yourself the height. Hold the spray can at a 45° angle to the panel (**fig 3**) — not at right angles or expellent gas rather than paint may be released, and could cause spatter. Try to keep the can-to-roof distance the same when you have to change position.

FACT FILE

Achieving a perfect match between old and new paintwork simply may not be possible, but there are a few tricks to try.

For **dark** or **dull** paint the best approach is to begin by polishing the area around the new paint with a cutting compound, such as T-Cut. Polishing the area around the repair will help blend the new paint in with the old. Alternatively, you can spray on a coat of aerosol clear lacquer over the new paint. This has the effect of darkening the newly sprayed area and should improve the match between old and new paintwork.

Faded paintwork is the hardest to match to new paint and there may be no alternative but to respray a whole panel. But check the paint manufacturer's colour charts to see if there is an alternative which better matches the faded colour than the original paint.

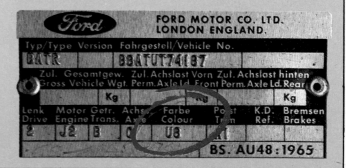

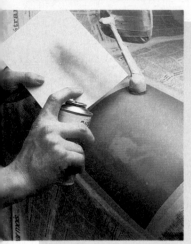

1. Spraying the primer

2. Rubbing down primer

The surface you intend to spray should be completely smooth, properly prepared and primed. This applies whether the surface is new, has been repaired, is being spruced up or is undergoing a colour change. Use a primer surfacer to start with so that you have a good surface for the top coat.

Primer surfacer is widely available in aerosol cans. Its job is to act as a seal between the raw surface of the panel or any filler, and the topcoat. It is also designed to provide a smooth keyed surface to which the top-coat firmly sticks. Spraying technique for primer is exactly the same as for the topcoat.

Spray on one coat of primer

3. Spraying on the first topcoat using card as a mask

FACT FILE

Where and when to spray

Aerosol spray paint almost always has to be used outside. Few home garages are big enough to move around in or have adequate ventilation. If you do spray indoors wear a mask, open windows and try not to breathe the fumes.

Choose a warm, still day for spraying. With even a light breeze, most of the spray will be blown away, or on to unmasked parts. Too cool or damp and the paint will 'bloom' — produce a dull, patchy finish. Always read the instructions on the can for recommended temperatures and conditions.

TIP

Aerosol economy

If you have any paint left over you can use it to touch up small stone chips in the bodywork. Rather than spraying a large area just to cover a small chip you can use it brushed on instead.

Direct the spray into a small container (such as the can lid) until you have enough for the job. Use a small, fine brush to apply it direct to the chip. Remember that it is thinner than normal brush paint, so you need more coats.

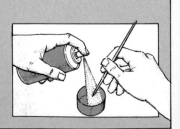

(**fig 1**) and allow 30 minutes to dry. Rub this down with well wetted 600 grade wet-and-dry paper (**fig 2**). If any imperfections are revealed fill them with cellulose putty — applied thinly with a plastic spatula or your fingers (see page 17). Next, spray on two more coats of primer, allowing 15 minutes between coats. Lightly rub the last coat with 800 then 1200 grade paper used wet. Rinse clean and allow to dry.

Now spray on the first of the topcoats (**fig 3**). Do not worry if the first coat looks patchy over the primer. Apply at least three more coats, allowing 15 minutes drying time between each. Four coats is the minimum for a fairly glossy shine but you can apply more for a deeper result.

If you get paint spatters on one of your topcoats — a common problem when the aerosol can is nearly empty — you will have to wait several days for the paint to harden before rubbing down the surface and respraying.

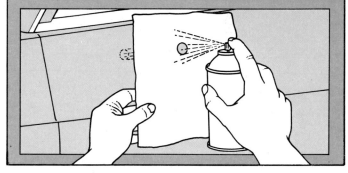
STEP 5 FINISH OFF

About 30 minutes after topcoating, carefully peel off the masking tape around the repaired area only. (Do not remove the tape from other areas at this stage.) Smooth down the topcoat with a cutting compound such as T-Cut (**fig 1**), paying special attention to any ridges that have built up next to the masking tape.

Now spray one final coat over both the repaired area and the immediately-adjacent paintwork. This will help the new paintwork blend in with the old.

Remove any paint that has got on to trim with a rag moistened with cellulose thinners. Take care not to spill any on new paintwork. Then remove any remaining masking tape.

The new paint may be brighter than surrounding areas, but these can be lifted to match (see Fact File box — Colour matching).

1. Smoothing down the topcoat

2. The finished result after polishing

Fault: Blooming (clouding of surface).

Cause: Weather too damp and cold for spraying.

Solution: Try using rubbing compound. If necessary rub down with wet paper and respray on a warmer day.

Fault: Topcoat shows up in bands and is not even.

Cause: Not enough overlap between strokes.

Solution: Flat down the surface with fine abrasive paper, used wet, and spray on more topcoats.

Fault: Ridging at edge of sprayed area.

Cause: Paint has built up in front of masking.

Solution: Rub down the ridge with fine paper used very wet. Respray the repair but do not spray close to masked parts.

Rustproofing your car

DIY rustproofing is cheap and simple to do. What's more, it both prolongs your car's life and increases its resale value

Rust damage sends more cars to the scrapyard than any other single cause. But although it is almost impossible to prevent a car from rusting altogether, there is a lot you can do to slow down the process.

You can treat a car of almost any age provided corrosion has not already taken strong hold. This generally involves coating the underbody with thick underseal and coating the inside of box sections — where rust often starts — with a proprietary rustproofing fluid or old engine oil.

Whether you want to make your own sprayer, as shown here, or use a bought type, the method of rustproofing is exactly the same.

When to do this job
Before serious rusting occurs

What this job involves
Cleaning the underside
Applying underseal
Rustproofing box sections, doors, boot and bonnet
Making a sprayer

Points to watch
Give all the rubber suspension bushes a squirt
of the wax as it will stop them cracking or squeaking
The excess will drip out so let the car stand on
some waste ground for a while

To do this job
Tools: Screwdrivers, wire brush; drill and drill bits (maybe) spanners (maybe); brush for underseal
Materials: Underseal; rustproofing kit; or old engine oil; garden sprayer; 40in. (1m) screenwasher tubing; Araldite; grommets or plastic plugs; masking tape
Time: Allow at least one day, preferably a weekend
Degree of difficulty: Very messy rather than difficult, especially when undersealing

If you have the job professionally done . . .
Has the underseal been properly applied to all areas? Have any access holes (if drilled) been plugged? Has all excess rustproofer been removed?

To do a good, long lasting job of protecting your car from rust it must be undersealed. The underside takes a constant pounding from stones and spray and corrosion can quickly take a hold.

There are two kinds of underseal — spray-on (in an aerosol can), and brush-on (**fig 1**). The spray-on type requires little effort to use but you must be careful not to spray the wrong parts. Brush-on underseal is more difficult to apply, but is cheaper than the aerosol type — particularly if you use a bitumastic compound, as sold for waterproofing roofing felt. This stays flexible and its rubbery surface resists stone chips better than ordinary underseal.

Before you use the underseal, all traces of dirt and rust must be cleaned off the underside of the floor panels. If you try to apply underseal over dirt, it will crack and peel off in a matter of weeks, and any moisture trapped under it will accelerate the rusting process.

Cleaning dirt off the underside is a messy job, so if you are going to do it yourself wear old clothes and make sure you

1. A selection of rustproofing kits and materials

wear goggles to protect your eyes from dirt.

Alternatively, you can have the car steam cleaned at a garage. This makes light work of cleaning the underside and exposes any rust, chipped paint or loose underseal. Failing that you can use a high pressure water lance — if your local garage car wash has one.

If you are cleaning the car at home, raise the car up as high as possible, making sure it is firmly supported on ramps or axle stands. If you have to work under cover be prepared for a lot of mess and make sure the work area is well ventilated.

If you are doing the job by hand, use a large stiff wire brush to remove all traces of mud and loose underseal (**fig 2**). Prise off any stubborn bits with a screwdriver then brush away any remaining loose material and wipe the surface over with a damp cloth.

Any areas of surface rust must be treated with a proprietary rust converter followed by a coat or two of primer.

If you find any rust holes in the

2. Removing dirt from sill using a wire brush

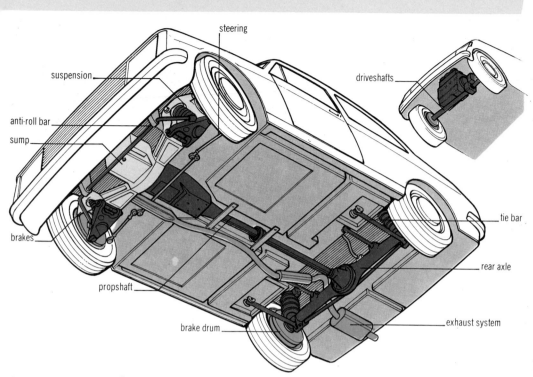

steering

suspension

anti-roll bar

sump

brakes

propshaft

brake drum

driveshafts

tie bar

rear axle

exhaust system

3. Use newspaper and masking tape to protect these areas — inset shows front wheel drive

floor or box sections they should be welded as the floorpan is usually structural.

When you are certain that all the rust has been treated you must protect all the parts which do not need undersealing (**fig 3**) with newspaper and masking tape. Also decide how far up the bodywork you want the underseal to go. The best place is on the line of a door sill and across the front and rear valances up as far as the bumper. This will protect the lower parts of the car from chips caused by stones.

When you have decided on your line, run a strip of masking tape all around the car, then use newspaper and more tape to mask the lower body (**fig 4**), not forgetting to mask the outside of the wheel arches. This is very important when using spray underseal. Make sure all the joins and tape runs are firmly stuck down.

4. Mask off the bodywork — ensure tape is firmly stuck down

Now you can apply the first coat of underseal. Apply one coat to the whole of the underside, taking care to brush or spray into all the nooks and crannies which can harbour rust. Pay special attention to the top and rear sections of front wings and the area around the headlights. This will not be too difficult if you are using spray-on underseal, but if you are using a brush, make sure you work the sealant well into all the corners. If necessary, remove the headlights and the grille

1. Brushing on the underseal — give sills a good coating

Whether you use a home made sprayer (see Tip — Make your own sprayer), or a ready made one in kit form, protecting the box sections is the same in both cases. The idea is to coat the inside with a rust preventer to protect the metal from moisture and water that builds up inside.

Rustproofing kits are oil containing wax which, when sprayed on, leaves a waxy skin over the metal. If you make your own sprayer you can buy the same rustproofing liquid to spray on. Alternatively, you can make your own from old engine oil, thinned with a little paraffin so it sprays easier, mixed with a non-acid rust inhibitor. If the oil is dirty, strain it first through an old stocking. This will take out the worst of the sludge and prevent the sprayer from blocking up.

The door sills are the most vulnerable part of the body to corrosion, as moisture often builds up inside them when the drain holes get blocked.

Most sills have an inner and an outer section, divided by a central diaphragm (**fig 1**). This means that the inner and outer sections have to be rustproofed individually — you cannot do both at the same time. The inner sill is the easiest to get at. If you are lucky you will not even have

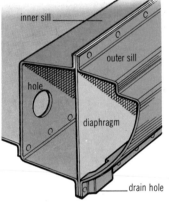

1. Cross-section through a sill

inner sill

outer sill

hole

diaphragm

drain hole

to drill any holes.

Begin by releasing the carpets where they fix to the sill. On nearly all cars you will have to unscrew plastic or metal holding strips while on others, which have the carpet glued into place, you will have to prise it away using a flat wide piece of wood. This should reveal holes (sometimes covered with tape) through which you can insert the sprayer's extension tube.

If there are no holes you will have to drill some in the sill. Use a drill just larger than the tube and drill three or four holes spaced out along the sill, plus one in each wheel arch.

Make your own sprayer

Making a sprayer with an extension tube for rust-proofing box sections and sills is cheap and easy and takes about an hour. You can make one out of an indoor plant sprayer, available from garden centres or hardware shops, and a few feet of windscreen washer tubing. The exact length of the tubing is not critical — just be sure to buy a length at least as long as the longest box section on your car.

Start by taking the nozzle off the sprayer. It should unscrew — if it is tight use pliers. Lay the nozzle face up on a work surface and, using a drill bit the same diameter as your screenwasher tubing, drill out the nozzle centre. Hold the nozzle tightly as you drill — use a vice or a pair of grips if you need to but take care not to crush the nozzle.

Take the piece of screen-washer tubing and push it through the hole to check for fit — it should fit very tightly. Now mix up some to help you get right into the crannies. Leave the first coat to dry for a couple of hours before you apply a second one.

Give all the areas exposed to stones and spray, such as the sills and wheel arches, an extra coat or two for added protection. Spray or brush right up to the edges of your masking, but do not apply the underseal too thickly on vertical faces or it will run and sag.

Leave the last coat to dry for a couple of hours, then peel off the masking tape. Once the

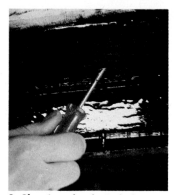

2. Clearing the drain holes

underseal has dried properly after two or three days, check for any areas you may have missed. Also, check that you have not blocked up drain holes in the sills and box sections. If you have, use a screwdriver or piece of coathanger wire to clear the obstructions (**fig 2**).

Once the job is complete all you have to do is to check the underside once a year for any signs of the underseal coming away and remove any build-up of road dirt with a soft brush and water from a hose.

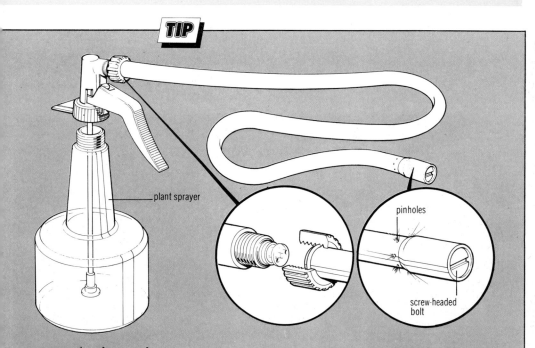

plant sprayer

pinholes

screw-headed bolt

epoxy resin glue, such as Araldite, and smear it round the end of the tube. Force the tube into the nozzle, wipe off any excess glue, and leave it to dry. Screw the nozzle and tube on the sprayer and then screw a tightly fitting short bolt into the other end of the tube.

Now use a pin to prick

holes in the tube — you will have to experiment a little until you get the spray pattern you want. If you find that you have made too many holes, simply cut the end off the tube, refit the bolt in and try again.

To test the spray, fill the bottle with old engine oil thinned with a little paraffin.

If the oil is especially dirty or gritty strain it through an old stocking — this will remove the worst of the lumps and avoid blocking the sprayer. Practise with the spray before you begin (see Tip — Even coverage) and when you are satisfied with the spray pattern you can treat the box sections.

Several lengths of tubing are supplied with most kits — some short and some long to reach into different box-sections. . Choose a piece long enough to reach right along to one end and feed the tube into the hole (**fig 2**) until it reaches the end of the sill. Now either pump the gun or depress the gun trigger to start spraying.

As you spray, slowly pull the tube back towards you to give the inside of the sill a good even coverage (See Tip — Even coverage). Stop spraying just as the tube comes out of the hole — any spillages can be wiped up using a cloth moistened with white spirit. Repeat the operation for each hole — the fluid or oil will run into all the areas of the sill. Do not worry if it drips out of the drain holes — it wipes off easily.

While the first sill is drying give the second one its first coat

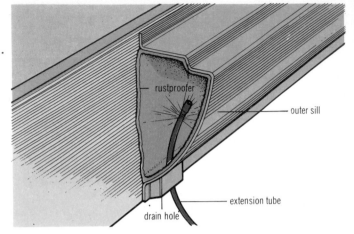

1. The extension tube covers the box section like this

of rustproofer. By the time you finish, the first sill will be ready for a second coat.

The outer sills are tackled differently. Find the drain holes and poke them clear with stiff

wire or a small screwdriver. Now see if the tube will fit through them. If it will, spray a coat of rustproofer as before. If not, you must drill holes to poke the probe through. Do not

2. Using the extension tube to get rustproofer right into the sill

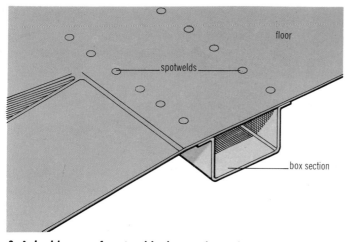

floor

spotwelds

box section

3. A double row of spotwelds shows where the box section is

4. Plugging hole with grommet

enlarge the drain holes — this could do more harm than good.

New holes are made in the top part of the sill, as you want to avoid drilling holes where water might get in. Use a drill just larger than the tube and drill carefully. If your car has sill kick plates remove them and drill the holes underneath. Apply two coats of rustproofer then plug the holes you have drilled with plastic plugs or rubber grommets (**fig 4**) available from accessory shops. You can paint them to match the car if you want.

Other box sections are treated in the same way — again, if there are no existing holes you must drill some. Be very careful when drilling near suspension mountings or steering mountings to avoid hitting any vital components.

Underbody crossmembers can be drilled from inside or outside. If you drill from inside, first check the position of the crossmember then take out the carpets and look for a double line of spotwelds, which look like small dents (**fig 3**) running across the floor. Drill carefully between the two lines and do not let the drill go through too far. Mark the depth required on the drill with a few turns of

insulating tape. Once you have drilled the holes, give each box section one, or preferably, two coats of rustproofer — cover the holes up with tape when you have finished.

If you drill from the outside make the hole away from road spray and remember to plug all the holes with grommets when you have applied the rustproofer.

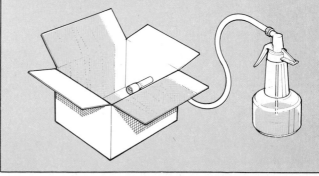

Most car doors tend to rust very badly along the bottom edge. This is caused by water which gets past the rubber seal at the bottom of the window glass remaining in the bottom of the door. Normally the water should drain out through holes in the door but these usually become blocked and then rust rapidly eats through from the inside, ruining the outer door skin and the lower part of the door itself.

There are several ways to get inside the doors. You may be able to fit your tubing through the drain holes — if so, use the extension tube to spray one coat all over the inside of the door. Make sure the window is wound up fully before you do this. Failing this, you can either drill your own holes in the door or try sticking the tube down past the window glass (**fig 1**) when it is wound down. This method may coat the window with rust-proofer so be prepared to wipe any mess off.

The last method involves taking off the door handles and trim pad, then peeling back the

1. Spraying inside the door past the window glass

plastic condensation sheet (**fig 2**), and spraying the inside using the sprayer's normal nozzle (**fig 3**). Once you have finished, make sure that you refit the plastic sheet, using gaffer tape

to make sure it is firmly fixed in place. Gaffer tape is a wide, very sticky, waterproof plastic tape which is widely available from most good hardware shops or motor factors. Once the

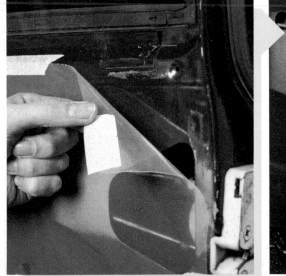

2. Peeling back the condensation sheet

3. Spraying rustproofer inside the door

4. Drilling the door pillar — masking tape stops drill slipping

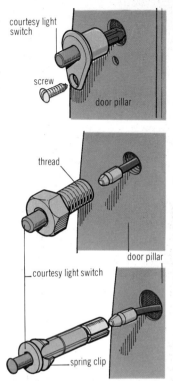

courtesy light switch

screw

door pillar

thread

door pillar

courtesy light switch

spring clip

5. Courtesy light switches are held in several ways

rustproofer has dried, use a small screwdriver or piece of coathanger wire to clear the door drain holes.

The door frames can also be treated. To get to these you can usually pull out or unscrew the courtesy light switches. **Fig 5** shows the most common fixings; otherwise drill a hole in the front and rear frames and spray through them.

One of the worst places for rust is the front and rear of the bonnet or bootlid. Some cars suffer more than others, especially those which have bracing box sections in the bonnet just above the radiator. The constant heating and cooling from the radiator creates condensation inside the box, which quickly leads to serious rusting of the box section. You can usually get at the inside of the sections through holes, otherwise you need to drill some. Be careful not to let the drill go too far or it may come through the outer panel. Give the sections two coats of rustproofer, making sure that it

covers all the inner surfaces (see Tip — Even coverage) and then leave it to dry.

Any fluid which oozes out can be wiped off with a rag soaked in white spirit.

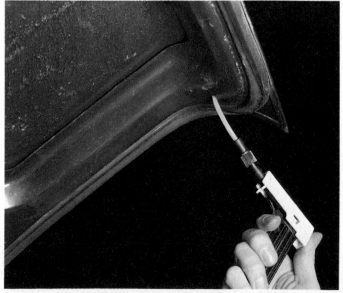

6. Using extension tube to reach into boot lid box sections

43

Fixing leaky weatherseals

Water leaking into the car interior is not just a nuisance — it can cause damage and promote rust. So tackle the problem as soon as any signs of a leak appear

Many owners only notice their weathersealing is leaking when the boot fills with water or their carpets get soggy underfoot. But the first signs of the problem may seem quite minor. Damp seats or door trims after a night's rain, unusually loud wind or road noise and un-explained draughts at high speed are all pointers that the time has come to renew the weatherseal.

Before you spend a lot of time inspecting the weatherstrip, check for other causes. Leaks can also be caused by ill-fitting doors and windows, or rust.

When to do this job
If water is getting inside the car, boot or bonnet

What this job involves
Repairing leaking door and window seals
Using silicone sealant
Repairing bonnet and boot seals

Points to watch
Rust often eats away the mountings flange for the windscreen along its bottom edge. If you get a new windscreen make sure the fitter uses plenty of sealant

To do this job
Tools: Pliers; flat-bladed screwdrivers; metal spoon (maybe); sealant applicator (maybe); knife (maybe); drill (maybe)
Materials: Chalk; scrap rubber (maybe); silicone sealant (maybe); new weatherstrip (maybe); self-adhesive draught excluder (maybe); grommets (maybe); contact adhesive (maybe)
Time: About an hour or two depending on the location of the leak
Degree of difficulty: Locating the leak can be tricky. Seal repair is generally straightforward

If you have the job professionally done . . .
Does the car still leak? Do all the doors and windows open and shut smoothly and easily?

Weatherstrips are sections or continuous pieces of rubber or felt which seal the space around the edges of doors, windows, boot-lids, tailgates and sunroofs. Shown below are the types normally fitted.

The most common type of weatherstrip fitted to doors and around boots consists of rubber tubing bonded to a plastic-coated metal channel. The same type of weatherstrip is fitted to the tailgates of hatchbacks and estates. Two main methods are used to fit the weatherstrip in place. In some cases, the strip is pressed on to a metal flange which runs around the door frame or boot aperture. In others, the strip is fitted into a V-shaped metal channel running around the inside of the door or boot.

Sliding or wind-up windows are held by U-shaped rubber or felt channels. These help to guide the windows and also prevent draughts and leaks.

Fixed windows — windscreens and rear windows, for example — are surrounded by a continuous rubber strip.

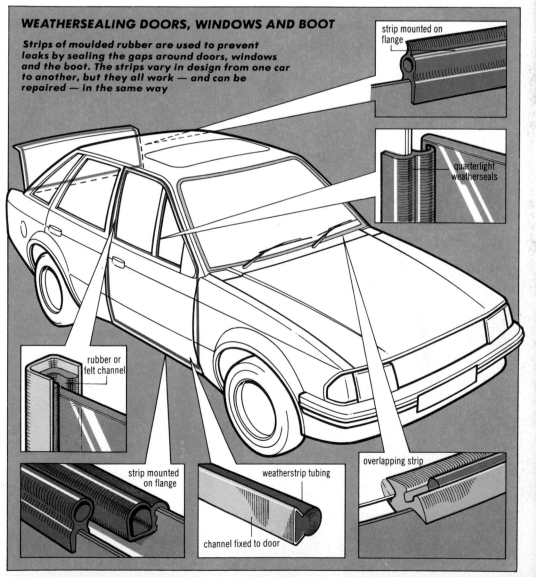

WEATHERSEALING DOORS, WINDOWS AND BOOT

Strips of moulded rubber are used to prevent leaks by sealing the gaps around doors, windows and the boot. The strips vary in design from one car to another, but they all work — and can be repaired — in the same way

strip mounted on flange

quarterlight weatherseals

rubber or felt channel

strip mounted on flange

weatherstrip tubing

channel fixed to door

overlapping strip

Having identified the weatherstrip the next step is to find the leak. Begin by checking the condition of the weatherstrip for obvious signs of damage. Loose, twisted or missing pieces are easily seen and will let in water. If nothing seems to be wrong, try pinching the strip with your fingers. Rubber hardens with age and becomes brittle, so splits and cracks develop. However, you should ignore the pinholes

1. Old weatherseals often show signs of wear and damage

STEP 3   REPAIR DOOR SEALS

If the leak is due to the bonded tubing type of weatherstrip not butting up properly to the door or the frame, prise off the faulty length and expose the flange it is mounted on (**fig 1**). Take great care here, as the flange is sometimes quite sharp. Gently tap the flange outwards along its whole exposed length, so that the weatherstrip will fit snugly against the door.

To refit the weatherstrip, first clench the channelling with pliers (**fig 3**) and squeeze the sides together for a tight fit, then press it back into place on the flange. At the corners, loop the channelling and push it on to the corner, then tap it gently

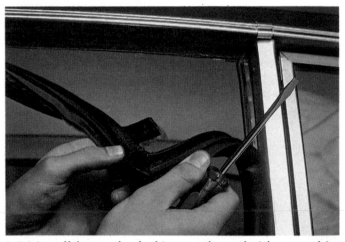

1. Prising off damaged or leaking weatherseal with a screwdriver

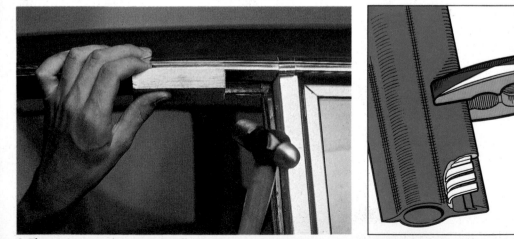

2. Flattening out the retaining flange to ensure a good fit

3. Squeezing the metal channel

found in some strips as these are deliberately intended to let air out when the door is closed.

If there is no obvious damage to the weatherstrip, dry the inside of the car thoroughly, then sit inside while someone pours or sprays water over the affected area. A garden hose pinched between the fingers or a watering can will do. It should be fairly easy to see where the water is coming in or where damp patches appear.

TIP

Chalk it

If you are working on your own, or if the leak is in the bonnet or boot, run chalk along the weatherstrip and repeat the water test. Let excess water drain away, then look at the strip. If the chalk mark has washed away anywhere, water is getting in at that point.

home with a rubber mallet or use the heel of your hand.

If the channelling or tubing is broken, it is possible to bridge it using a length of rubber cut from an inner tube (**fig 4**). Roll the rubber into a tube and insert it into the broken ends of the weatherstrip tubing. Where there is a gap between the broken ends, it may be necessary to glue it into place with an impact adhesive (**fig 5**). Refit the channelling and cover the repair with tape (**fig 6**).

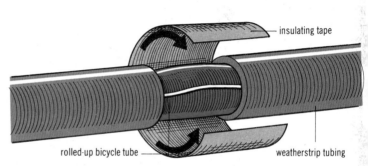

insulating tape

rolled-up bicycle tube

weatherstrip tubing

4. Repairing a broken weatherstrip using an old bicycle tube

5. Coating broken ends with impact adhesive

6. Covering the repair with insulating tape

On wind-up or sliding windows, the U-shaped channels which surround the windows often become damaged and leak.

On wind-up windows it should be possible to remove the damaged section and renew it with a fresh piece. If, on in-spection, you find that a large area is affected, it may be better to renew the entire channel.

Lever the channelling free with a screwdriver and pull it away from the metal surround (**fig 1**). Trim off the damaged section with a sharp knife and cut a new piece to fit.

Before you refit the channel-ling, cover the back of both lengths with impact adhesive (**fig 2**). Make sure that the new section lines up exactly with the existing channelling, otherwise the window may not open and

1. Prising out the felt or rubber insert

2. Coating the new channel with adhesive

Windscreen and fixed windows often give trouble on older cars. Fortunately, if the rubber seals of these windows are leaking, they can easily be resealed with a silicone sealant.

Water seeping from the bottom of a window may actually be entering at the top and running down the sides. If you cannot see exactly where the leak is try using the chalk test (see Tip — Chalk it). So it is best to reseal the whole surround (**fig 1**).

Start in the centre of the rubber at the top outer edge. Lever up the rim with a metal spoon handle (**fig 2**). Insert the nozzle of the sealant applicator and smoothly squeeze the sealant under the rim (**fig 3**). Then slowly draw the nozzle along the top and halfway down the side. Work plenty of sealant into the corners, as these are the most vulnerable areas. Now go to the bottom outer edge of the rubber in the centre and work back halfway up the side. Be sure to overrun the point where you stopped before.

Go back to the top centre, but this time lever up the rubber against the glass. Do not worry about damaging the glass — it is tougher than the tools you are using. Squeeze in the sealant as before, working halfway down the side and then starting at the bottom centre.

Now seal the other half of the window, following the above sequence. When you have finished, use a blunt knife to remove excess sealant which has strayed on to the glass.

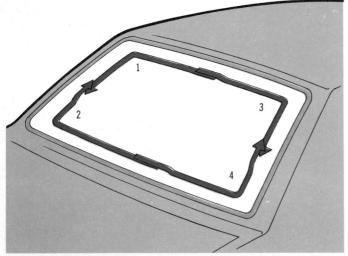

1. Sealing fixed windows — correct order of work

close properly. Leave the glue to set for a few hours before operating the window.

Leaking channelling on sliding windows can be patched up in the same way. But if the entire channel is affected, it should be renewed, including the lower section which acts as a runner for the glass.

To do this, first unscrew and remove the window catches and the retaining strip fixed to the inside of the door (**fig 3**). Then lift out the glass.

Check the side and top channelling for damage and repair or replace it as described above. Prise away the lower channelling and unscrew and remove the U-shaped metal surround below. Cut a new metal surround to length and drop it into place. Drill fixing

3. Component parts of a typical sliding window

holes in the metal surround and screw it in place. You may have to use slightly larger gauge screws for a tight fit. Cut the felt channel to size and push it into

the surround. Then refit the glass and retaining strip. Finally screw the catches back into place and check that the window works smoothly.

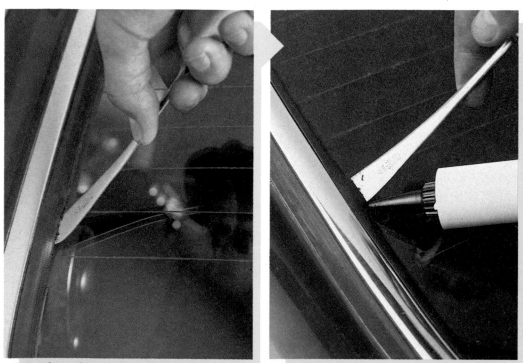

2. Lifting the weatherseal with a spoon

3. Squeezing sealant under the rim

Where the door trims are damp and you have repaired the door seals and window channels as described in Step 3 and 4, check the metal/rubber strips fixed to the door where the glass emerges. These expand and lose their tension as they get older and let water inside the door (**fig 1**).

Also check the drain holes along the bottom edge of the door. If these are blocked, clear them with a piece of stiff wire.

If it proves impossible to clear the drain holes, or if the metal/rubber strips need renewing, you will have to strip down the trim and winder mechanism (this is covered in another article).

Quarterlights are small triangular windows usually found in the corner of door window frames, which hinge independently of the main winding window.

The most common cause of a leak in an opening quarterlight is a faulty catch.

The catch on the quarterlight ensures that there is a pressure fit between the glass and the rubber. However, the rubber sometimes gives with age, and a gap appears. If the catch is non-adjustable, cut a short length of self-adhesive foam rubber (draught excluder) and fit it to the frame to fill the gap (**fig 2**).

If there is still a leak, seal it as described in Step 4.

1. Damaged metal and rubber window strips

2. Sealing the quarterlight with adhesive strip

Weatherstrip is sometimes fitted at the rear of the bonnet opening, or around the boot or tailgate. Test for leaks using the chalk method, and if any leaks appear, remove the weatherstrip and adjust the mounting flange as in Step 1.

Where there is damp in the boot but the weatherstrip and channels do not appear to be causing it, check the boot lock, the trim, and any badges for fit (**fig 1**). If these are loose or missing, either tighten them up or renew them, as water could be getting in through their mounting holes.

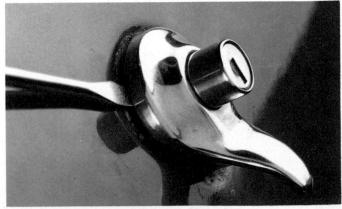

1. Testing for leaks around poorly fitting locks

Replacing a bolt-on wing

If you have a corroded or crumpled wing and it is the bolt-on type, replacement is a simple job that can be done in a day

Due to rising insurance costs, car manufacturers are being forced to make their cars easier to repair. One way they are doing this is to fit bolt-on panels instead of welded ones. This reduces labour time and therefore, the cost of repair.

What this job involves
Removing all the trim fitted to the wing
Unbolting the old wing
Tackling any further rust
Fitting the new wing
Replacing the trim
Checking and road testing

Points to watch
Most cars are now fitted with bolt-on wings
Always check both sides of the inner wing flitch plate before starting work as bad rust here must be repaired before you fit the new wing
Is it worth getting a full respray instead of just painting the new wing?

To do this job
Tools: Crosshead screwdriver; socket spanner with short extension and ratchet handle; hacksaw or cold chisel and hammer; open ended spanner or straight ring spanner
Materials: Wing; mastic sealer; dismantling fluid; rust killer and primer; underseal; bumper bolts and trim fastenings (maybe); light lubricating oil
Time: A day allowing for dealing with rust under wing and repainting with primer
Degree of difficulty: Can be very difficult to take the old fixing bolts out; aligning new wing needs care

If you have the job professionally done . . .
Is the wing lined up properly and are all the gaps around it even? Is the headlamp aligned properly? Does the new paint match and is it free from runs? Have all traces of mastic sealant been removed?

Bolt-on wings are attached to the main body and inner wings by a number of bolts or screws, rather than by a series of spot welds. To check if your car has bolt-on front wings, open the bonnet and look along the side edge of the engine compartment where the bonnet fits — normally referred to as a drip rail. If you can see a row of screws or bolt heads in the channel where the inner and the outer wings meet, (**fig 1**), then the wing is bolted on.

It is less common for rear

1. To identify bolt-on wings, look for bolt heads like this

Prices for replacement wings vary widely so it is well worth shopping around. If you buy from your main dealer you will almost certainly pay more but you will be sure to get a wing that matches the original in quality and fit. Much better deals are, however, often obtainable from specialist suppliers. Sometimes these firms stock wings which they buy direct from the car maker, but more often they manufacture their own *pattern parts* that is, copies of the original. Most professionals use pattern parts and providing you buy from a reputable supplier you can be sure that the new wing will be well made and fit properly.

Some suppliers also advertise fibreglass replacement wings which offer considerable savings. Fibreglass wings do, however, suffer from a number of drawbacks. They can be difficult to finish to the same standard as the rest of the car, cheaper ones are prone to crazing when hit or leant on, and the use of fibreglass wings or any other fibreglass body panels will almost certainly devalue your car.

If you don't mind doing a little

1. A badly damaged wing and bolt-on replacement

2. Straightening flanges

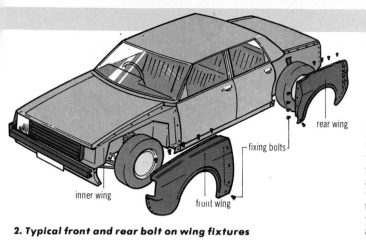

wings to be bolted on although some cars such as VW Beetles, Morris Minors, the Rover 2000 and some Citroëns do have them. To check whether on your car the rear wings are bolted on, you will first have to clean off some of the mud from inside the wheel-arch. This will be easier with the wheel off. Then look for the flange of the wing standing away from the rest of the body-work and a row of bolts holding the flange to the main body. If your car is like this, your wings are bolted on.

2. Typical front and rear bolt on wing fixtures

extra work the cheapest way to get a new wing is to buy one from a car breaker. However, make sure that the wing is genuinely in good condition before you go to the trouble of taking it off. Bear in mind that cars of the same model tend to rust in the same places so if you are replacing a wing because of rust damage check the 'new' wing very carefully for similar signs of corrosion.

If your local scrapyard will not remove the wing you must take great care when unbolting it to ensure that you do not damage it

(see Step 4). There are often metal flanges around the headlamps that have to be kept in alignment and care must be taken not to twist the wing or bend its flanges. If the flanges or the fixing straps are slightly bent or damaged you can bend them into line using Mole grips, pliers or even an adjustable spanner (**fig 2**). If the flanges are badly bent you may have to knock the wing into shape. Use a light hammer otherwise you might misalign the whole wing. If you are forced to hammer the wing, hold a block of wood

against the back of the wing to act as an anvil (**fig 3**).

Finally, whether you are fitting a new or secondhand wing, make sure that the wing is clean inside and out and com-pletely free from rust. Then apply a couple of coats of rust resisting primer followed by underseal on the inside of the wing (**fig 4**). Despite the fact you may scratch or chip the wing during fitting, both these jobs are much easier to do while the wing is off the car. Any small areas of damage can be touched up before the respray.

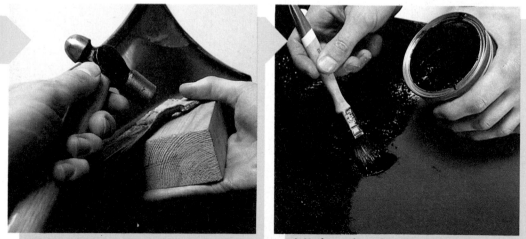

3. Using a hammer to tap flanges straight

4. Undersealing the new wing

In most cases, the first thing you will have to do is to take off the bumper. Most bumper bolts are like coach bolts so that the nut can be undone without the need to hold the bolt. But if the nut is

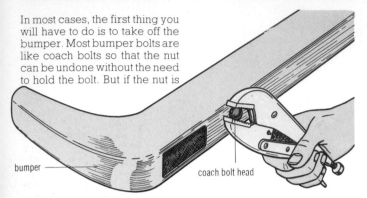

bumper

coach bolt head

1. Preventing a coach bolt from turning, using Mole grips

rusted on or the bumper has been damaged, the bumper bolt may just turn round when you turn the nut. If this happens, hold the domed end with Mole grips and try again (**fig 1**). Use a hacksaw if this does not work.

At the front the bumper will be bolted to the bumper irons. The bumper irons are very strong so if the nuts are rusted on badly and there seems to be no way that you can remove them, you can safely use a cold chisel and hammer to split the nut at the thinnest part if this will save time (**fig 3**). Make sure that the chisel is quite sharp and use a heavy

hammer. Alternatively, hacksaw through the nut or bolt. Obviously if you use either of these methods you will have to buy new nuts or bolts.

The side mounting for the bumper is usually attached straight on to the wing and this is even more likely to be rusted into place. If the side fixing is well rusted in and all other attempts to free it fail, use a hacksaw to cut through the bolt, or use the hammer and cold chisel to cut the wing away.

On some cars the wing can be unbolted once you have removed the bumper. On

others, further trim will need to be removed. Look at your new wing and note the position of the bolt holes — you should then be able to see what else has to come off. Many of the bolts will be in awkward places and you will usually have at least to remove the headlamp.

Round headlamps often have a chrome bezel which must come off first. The bezel is usually fitted with a crosshead screw at its base and once this is removed the bezel can be prised off. Otherwise the snap-off type just needs a screwdriver blade inserted gently behind to prise it away. Sometimes the grille acts as a bezel as well, so you may have to remove it first to get access to the headlamp retaining screws. The grille will be held to the body by a number of clearly visible crosshead screws.

On older cars with large headlamps the headlamp bowl is held to the wing by three or four crosshead screws. With these screws removed, the whole unit can be removed in one piece. But on the smaller headlamps mounted in pairs there is usually a further chrome ring which must be removed, followed by the light unit itself. Only then can you get to the screws which secure the headlamp bowl to the wing.

Where the headlamp is mounted flush with the bodywork, check behind it to see if the adjusters hold the headlamp in. There may be nuts below the adjusters which must be removed. Otherwise the headlamp may be held in by separate nuts and washers or even by springs which simply have to be pulled off the casing. Once the light unit is out, pull the electrical wiring back into the engine compartment where it will not be damaged. Usually the headlamp bowl itself is held on to its mounting flange with crosshead screws and spring clips. The bowl itself may need to be

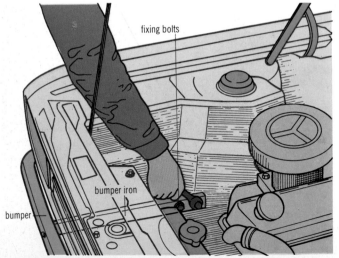

fixing bolts

bumper iron

bumper

2. Undo the bumper iron bolts to get the bumper off

3. Splitting a seized nut with a cold chisel

4. Removing the headlight unit from wing

treated for rust and repainted. It is, however, probably easier and more effective to renew a rusted headlamp bowl as they are not very expensive. The panel supply firm who sold you the bolt-on wing may also be able to supply the standard headlamp bowl in metal or plastic — here it is worth going for the plastic type.

Sidelights and indicator units are other items usually fixed with crosshead screws or bolts. In most cases it is just a matter of removing the screws that protrude from the lens and pulling the whole unit out of the wing. If that does not work, remove the lens after removing its screws (**fig 5**) — the light unit fixing screws will then be easy to see. Having taken out the lamp unit, trace the wiring back until you come to a connector in the engine compartment. Separate the connector and leave the fixed wiring safely in the engine compartment.

Wing mirrors and aerials are often the most difficult components to get off the wing.

Their securing nuts are often hard to get at and often become very clogged with mud. Instead of taking hours removing them in the normal way, it may be easier to simply leave them in place until the wing is off the car and then cut around the base of the fitting with a cold chisel and

hammer, a hacksaw or even a pair of tin snips if you have them. Then you can clean the area underneath the fitting and use a dismantling spray to help move the obstinate parts. If the fixings prove really difficult to move, clamp the items carefully in a vice and use a wrench.

5. Take off the sidelight lens, then remove the unit itself

Before you start the job, examine the wing fixing bolts. If the bolts holding the wing on look really rusty, apply penetrating oil or releasing fluid to them every couple of days for a week or so before you do the job. When you come to remove the bolts they should then undo without too much difficulty.

If the wing is really rusty you may be able to tear it off its bolts with your bare hands. If any of the bolts prove awkward, try cutting through them with a hammer and chisel or a hacksaw. If this treatment does not work, see Tip, Clipped wings, or drill the head off the bolt. If you have an electric drill this is probably the easiest method. First, centre punch the bolt head to stop the drill slipping. Then, using a small drill, bore a hole right through the head. Next, take a drill slightly larger in diameter than the threaded part of the bolt. Drill in the same way with this and the bolt head will come away. Drill the piece of broken bolt out of the hole. You will have to use a new bolt and nut when you fit the new wing.

If you are in any doubt about where all the fixing bolts are, check on the new panel. Some

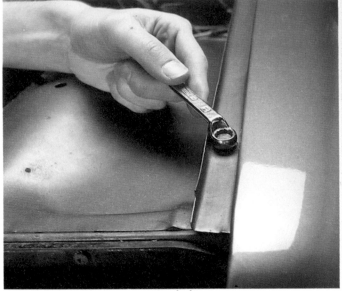

1. Undoing a wing top mounting bolt

Exposed

With most cars the wing fixing bolts will be obscured by a layer of underseal or mastic. This will stop you from getting a socket or a spanner fully on to the bolt head. However, you can get around the problem by cutting away the mastic first with a utility knife.

The new wing, when fitted, will only be as strong as the metal that you are bolting it to. Look around the inner wing, the suspension mounting points and up the door post to make sure that rust has not damaged the structure of the car. There should be no obvious holes or serious rust within 12 in. (300 mm) of any suspension mounting point. If everything is sound with only normal surface rusting, clean the area with a wire brush (**fig 1**) and apply a coat of rust resisting primer and some underseal (**fig 2**).

If any area is badly weakened

1. If the inner wing is rusty clean it with a wire brush

Clipped wings

If you have difficulty in undoing any of the wing fixing bolts, for example where the bolts or the wing are very rusty and inaccessible, simply cut the wing off with a hammer and cold chisel or a pair of tinsnips. You will not need the wing again so it does no harm to be brutal.

Once you have cut the wing off, leaving the fixing bolts in place, you will be able to get spanners to each end of the bolts, making removal easy.

of the bolts around the headlamp and the door pillar can be difficult to find and undo. An open-ended spanner is ideal for these areas where a socket can not be used. Otherwise a ring spanner with or without the usual bend is the one to use. Do not be afraid to cut or bend the old wing if it will help you to get access to the bolts.

The fixing bolts will be covered in paint and the threads will usually be rusty. Remove the paint around the head with a sharp screwdriver and pay particular attention if the fixing is a crosshead screw.

If you have space, the best tool to use is a small socket spanner, preferably one of the slim types based on a 3/8 in. drive. Make sure that you get an exact fit. If you have any difficulty in removing the bolts, do not waste time being gentle. Try an angle grinder if all else fails.

2. After removing any rust, underseal the inner wing

by rust, in most cases you will have to get a professional to weld in some strengthening plates. Special plates are made fo fit problem areas on many cars, so check whether the panel supplier stocks them. Making up your own repair panels and welding them in is covered in a subsequent article.

Before fitting the new wing, put some oil or grease on the threads of the fixing bolts to make reassembly easier. This will also help if you need to remove the wing again for any reason.

1. Checking to see that the new wing fits correctly

2. Applying mastic sealer

Bolting the new wing on is often the easiest part of the job. First offer the wing up to the body (**fig 1**) and make sure that all the flanges and brackets are exactly right. If not, bend them carefully until they all line up.

Once you are satisfied, run a bead of mastic sealer, available from good DIY stores, on to the main bodywork wherever the wing will come into contact with it (**fig 2**). This seals the joint.

Ask an assistant to hold the wing in place while you start to bolt it on, working from the bottom upwards. Put the first few bolts in loosely, say all the bottom ones, plus a couple along the top of the wing (**fig 3**) and one in the door pillar. Oil or grease the bolt threads before you start them off.

Now check that the door shuts correctly and the bonnet sits properly in the drip rail. Shut the door very carefully at first to avoid damaging it if the wing is not aligned properly. Try to get the gaps between the panels even and a smooth line along the side where the wing and the door meet. Check also that any ridges or pressings in the metal run straight along the wing and line up with the door.

When you are sure that everything is in line, tighten up

3. Fitting one of the wing top fixing bolts

4. Removing excess sealer

the bolts already in place and then fit all the others. Use a rag or scraper to remove the surplus mastic (**fig 4**).

With the wing in place you can now refit the headlamp assembly, bumper and any other ancillaries which were removed. Having taken the trouble to fit a new wing it is worth making sure that everything is correctly assembled with new gaskets (if fitted) and screws all correctly in place so that no further deterioration takes place.

Replace any bulbs that are showing signs of blackening and clean up the electrical terminals as you assemble them. If any of the screws seem not to bite properly you can replace them with slightly bigger ones, or fit a new fastener which they screw into.

If, when refitted, the bumper does not appear to be straight, put some large washers between it and the bumper iron to bring it into line. If the bumper irons are obviously bent, they can either be levered back straight or replaced, as most types bolt to the front chassis members. You can bend a bumper iron by slipping a length of heavy gauge tubing over it and levering it. Make sure you line up the bumper correctly as nothing will spoil the job more than a bumper that is out of line. Do up the wing fixing on the bumper last and put a rubber packing between the wing and the bumper to prevent damage to the paint-work — you can cut down a large grommet for this.

If you do not want to go to the trouble of fitting a wing mirror, door mounted ones are easier to fit. But if you want to keep your wing mirror, either align the mirror with the one on the other wing or ask someone else to help you establish the position which gives you the best field of view. Mark the best spot and cover it and the surrounding area with masking tape, then drill the hole carefully. Grease the thread after fitting the nut and protect the stalk left

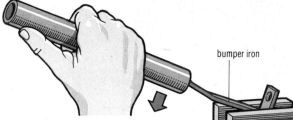

1. Straightening bumper iron

sticking out under the wing with a piece of hose or rubber pipe to keep the water out.

Having fitted the wing, you will need to paint it if it does not already match the car — spray painting is covered in another article. The headlights will almost certainly need adjusting now, so check their aim up against a fence or a blank wall.

Finally, listen out for any unusual rubbing or scraping sounds which could indicate that the new wing is fouling the wheel — especially when cornering or braking. Also examine the brake hoses carefully. Check that they are not being damaged by the wing.

2. Feed wiring back from engine compartment

3. New wing ready for respray

Are you sitting comfortably?

Seat adjusters which work reliably and smoothly make your car more comfortable and help you to find a safe driving position

All modern cars have mechanisms for adjusting the seats. After a time these adjusting devices can get clogged with dirt, rusted in one place or just worn out. Once you have taken the seat out of the car, many repairs to seat adjusters are a simple matter of cleaning and lubricating so that the seat can run smoothly.

Some parts of the seat's adjusters, such as the reclining mechanism, are sometimes sealed units so that you cannot mend them but need to replace them with new units. In this case it can be worth going to a car breaker where you may be able to buy the parts you need or even a complete seat which you can transfer to your car.

When to do this job
When seats do not slide freely on runners
When seats are loose
When seats do not recline properly

What this job involves
Checking seat runners
Fastening seat mountings
Removing seats
Fixing sliding mechanisms
Fixing reclining mechanisms
Fixing seat back release mechanisms

Points to watch
If you decide on a replacement seat from a scrapyard hunt around for one from the top of the range
Check that none of the springs in the seat base are disconnected

To do this job
Tools: Spanners; wire brush, hammer; pliers; Allen key (maybe); old toothbrush
Materials: Grease; penetrating oil; degreasing fluid; general purpose adhesive (maybe); new cable release, reclining mechanism and spacers (maybe)
Time: Up to two hours
Degree of difficulty: Bolts may be rusted; some parts of reclining mechanism may be difficult to reach

Before you begin removing the seat from the car, first check whether you can make the repair with the seat in place. If the seat feels loose on its runners, for instance, it may well be that the bolts holding the runners to the floor have worked their way loose. You should be able to reach under the seat with a spanner to tighten all the bolts (**fig 1**). In some cases you will find that there are locking nuts fitted to the underside of the car so you will need two spanners.

Many modern cars have runners which are combined with the seat frame and the entire seat and runner assembly is held in place by brackets. Check that the brackets are in good condition and show no signs of corrosion or distortion. Make sure that

their bolts are tight.

Your seat may feel slightly loose on its mountings and may swivel slightly from side to side. Some manufacturers design their seat mountings so that only one of the fixing bolts fastens through a circular hole in the runner and into a captive nut. The other bolts pass through slots so that you can adjust the angle of the seat slightly. Find the most suitable seat position and then tighten up all the bolts.

Another problem which can be solved easily with the seat still in the car happens when the runners become blocked so that the seat no longer slides backwards and forwards smoothly. The most common culprit is the carpet which is often a loose fit around the seat base and may have got caught in the runners. Check that this

has not happened — usually the best way to get at the runner is by looking under the seat from behind in the passenger compartment. If the carpet seems to be the cause of the problem, instead of just pulling it out of the way it may be a good idea to stick it down with a general purpose adhesive.

If the inside of your car ever gets wet — perhaps through a leaking window seal or a rust hole — you may find that floor mounted runners have rusted so that the seat no longer runs smoothly or will not even run backwards and forwards at all. You may be able to reach under the seat with a small wire brush and clean the rust off the runners before giving them a coating of grease. However, it is more than likely that you will have to take the seat out.

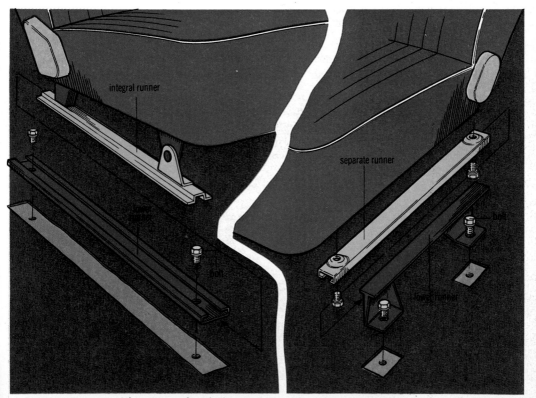

1. Seat runners are either integral with the seat or can be removed separately

Make sure that the runners are not blocked with any debris. Try cleaning the runners out with a paintbrush or, better still, an old toothbrush (**fig 1**). Once they are clean, put a little grease on them to make the seats move more smoothly.

Some seats which are attached to the floor by their runners have plastic spacers which fit between the seat and the runners or between the runners and the floor (**fig 2**). There is a spacer or group of spacers for each bolt holding the runners in place — usually one at each end. These spacers tend to split and break apart so that one corner of the seat

1. Using a toothbrush to clear dirt from the runners

If you find that you cannot make the necessary repair with the seat still in place, you will have to take the seat out of the car.

There are several different methods used for attaching a front seat to the floor. With one fixing arrangement the whole of the seat's frame is bolted to the floor. Another type uses a bracket which clamps the front of the seat's frame to the floor and allows the entire seat to pivot forward to let passengers into the back seat. With this type there is usually a catch which holds the rear of the seat to the floor of the car.

Whichever type is used on your car it should be easy to identify and unbolt the brackets which hold the seat in place (**fig 1**). The bolts sometimes go straight into the floorpan and

1. Removing the bolts which hold the seat to the floor

often become rusted into place. If this happens, do not try and force the bolt with a socket spanner — you will probably shear the head off. Instead tap the bolt smartly with a hammer several times and soak the area with penetrating oil. If you can see the threads from underneath the car, spray penetrating oil there as well.

Once you have taken off the fixing bracket or brackets, you should be able to lift the seat out of the car, although in cases where the seat is designed to tilt forward you will have to release the catch which holds the rear of the seat to the floor. If the seat has a reclining mechanism, tilt the seat as far forward as

TIP

Bolthole

The bolts that fasten the seat runners may get lost under the carpet if you leave them lying around so screw them loosely back into their threaded holes after you have taken them out of the seat mountings.

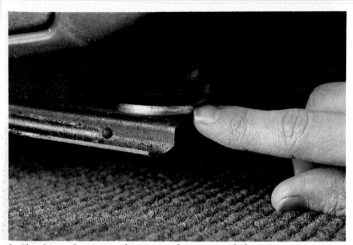

suddenly begins to sag and feels very loose.

New spacers should be available from your local dealer, but if you have any problems buying them you will have to improvise with something the same size but made of steel.

It is an easy job to fit the new spacers in place. Simply push the seat forward or backward so that you can gain more access to the area around the spacer. Use a spanner or a socket spanner to loosen the bolt from the floor. In some cases you will find that a bolt with a recessed hexagon is used so you will need an Allen key to loosen it.

2. Checking the spacer between the seat and the runner

possible to make it easier to lift out of the car.

The seats may also be held to the floor by their runners which are not an integral part of the seat. Seats of this type may have locking pins or nuts on the front of their runners to prevent the seat from going too far forward. Once you have taken these pins out of their locating holes or removed the bolts the seat can be pushed all the way forward until it comes off its runners. Other cars have nothing apart from the control lever to stop the seat going all the way forward until it comes off the runners so this type is easy to remove.

However, often the easiest way to remove a seat held in place by its runners is to unbolt the runners completely so that the seat and the runners can be lifted out as a single unit.

Begin by sliding the seat all the way forward so that you can take the rear bolts out of the runners. Make a note of any washers or spacers that are fitted. Now slide the seat all the way backwards so that the front bolts can be removed and then lift the whole seat assembly away.

Captive nuts

Some cars have bolts which fasten into *captive* or *caged* nuts. Where a captive nut fastening is used, the nut is enclosed by a pressed sheet metal box so that it cannot turn. This means that you do not need to hold the nut while you turn the bolt. If this metal box surrounding the nut has corroded away, you may be able to get a spanner on to the nut to stop it from turning. A problem may arise if you have not got the right spanner to fit on to a square captive nut. If so, use an adjustable spanner or self-locking grips.

If the captive nut has come loose but cannot be reached because it is inside a box section, you may be able to cut or drill the bolt to unfasten it. You can then replace the bolt with a toggle bolt, available from a DIY shop, which pushes through the hole and then spreads out on the other side so that the wings of the toggle prevent it turning round when you tighten the bolt. The most common reason for a captive nut to fail is rust. Have a look at the area around the nut to see if some bodywork repair is needed.

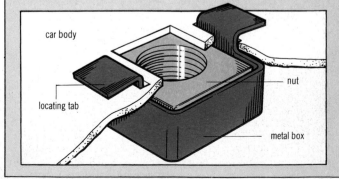

If you were having difficulty sliding the seats backwards and forwards you may find that this was caused by badly corroded runners. If the car is only driven by one person it can often happen that after a few years the runners get so rusty and dirty that it becomes impossible to move the seat. A wire brush will probably clean away any rust, but the runners may benefit from being cleaned in paraffin (kerosene) or a proprietary degreasing fluid such as Gunk (**fig 1**). Once they are clean and dry, coat the runners with grease and check that the release mechanism works properly.

The runners also have a spring mechanism which should lock the seat firmly in place and prevent any movement backwards or forwards — this is usually a 'tooth and dog' mechanism. This consists of a series of slots or 'teeth' cut into the runners at regular intervals. A peg or 'dog' is fixed to one side of the slotted runner. A strong spring fastened to the peg forces it to engage with the nearest tooth to lock the seat in place. The dog can be disengaged by operating a lever — this is either mounted

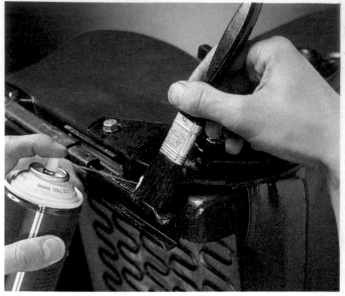

1. Using a degreaser aerosol to clean the seat runners

on the side of the seat or is operated remotely by a control on the front of the seat.

If the seat is jammed in place, first try the lever itself to see if it is jammed. You may find that you can free it with penetrating oil. Often parts like this seize up through lack of use.

Alternatively, the lever which pulls the dog out of the tooth may be loose or broken. On many cars this lever cannot be renewed as a separate item, but on others it can be removed by disengaging its return spring and then undoing the bolt or circlip which holds it in place. This is the sort of part which may be easier to find in a breaker's yard than at your local dealer.

The opposite problem — where the seat keeps sliding backwards and forwards and will not stay locked in place — is likely to be caused by the spring which is supposed to hold the dog in the engaged position. It may have broken or have come away from the lever. Use a pair of needle nose pliers to fasten the spring back into the correct position.

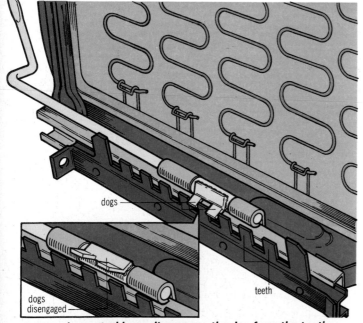

dogs

dogs disengaged

teeth

2. How the control lever disengages the dog from the teeth

INDEX

Bold entries indicate subjects covered in detail